MW00586886

I'll See You Again, Lady Liberty

The True Story of a German Prisoner of War in America

by

Ernst W. Floeter

with

Lynne Breen

WingSpan Press

Published in the United States and the United Kingdom

by WingSpan Press, Livermore, CA

The WingSpan name, logo and colophon are the trademarks of
WingSpan Publishing.

ISBN 978-1-59594-536-5

First edition 2014

Printed in the United States of America

www.wingspanpress.com

Publisher's Cataloging-in-Publication Data

Floeter, Ernst W.
I'll see you again, Lady Liberty : the true story of a German prisoner
of war in America / Ernst W. Floeter ; with Lynne Breen.
pages cm
ISBN: 978-1-59594-536-5 (pbk.)
1. Prisoners of war—Biography. 2. German Americans—
Biography. 3. World War, 1939-1945—Prisoners and prisons,
American. 4. Prisoners of war—United States—History—20th
century.   I. Breen, Lynne. II. Title.
D805.U5 F56 2014
940.54`8143—dc23
                                                        2014943882

1 2 3 4 5 6 7 8 9 10

Per aspera ad astra

Through hardships to the stars

Table of Contents

Prologue: Making a Wish 1

Chapter One: "Heil Hitler, You Fat Swine!" 3

Chapter Two: They Never Talked About It 7

Chapter Three: Blood and Honor 13

Chapter Four: Praying for Deliverance 16

Chapter Five: They Would Not See the End of the War 21

Chapter Six: Mortar Shells Straight at Us 27

Chapter Seven: "The Amis Are Here!" 32

Chapter Eight: Crackers with a Splendid Jam 38

Chapter Nine: Kissing Europe Goodbye 42

Chapter Ten: The Chance of a Lifetime 48

Chapter Eleven: "Have You Had Your Candy Already?" 53

Chapter Twelve: The Art of Picking Cotton 58

Chapter Thirteen: Censorship on Both Sides 64

Chapter Fourteen: "Thank Heavens, It's Over!" 70

Chapter Fifteen: Like Free People 75

Chapter Sixteen: A Country in Chaos 79

Chapter Seventeen: "Don't Forget Your Homeland" 84

Chapter Eighteen: Small-Town America 90

Epilogue: My Guardian Angel 96

Glossary: Selected Terms of World War II 100

Prologue

Making a Wish

On September 1, 1939, when the German Army marched into Poland, the beginning of the end of Nazi Germany had just begun. With the Great War ending only a generation before, no one could imagine that yet another war, which would go down in history as World War II, would last in Europe until 1945.

Either Germany would win this conflict, as many believed, or end in utter defeat, with the destruction of many German cities and the loss of our eastern provinces to Poland.

Since there was no other way of ridding the world of the Nazi menace, Germany had to lose unless a miracle happened—a revolt by German patriots—before everything was ruined. But as the world would learn, such a revolt was not to be. Adolf Hitler had a pact with the devil, who saved him from all of the plots against his life.

Germany was destined to pay a high price for the atrocities carried out by Hitler's Gestapo, not only in Germany, but also in Poland and the other occupied countries.

I grew up in the city of Stettin, the capital of the province of Pomerania, the largest German seaport on the Baltic Sea, northeast of Berlin. Sitting together with friends in the evening, expecting an air raid by the Polish air force on that first day of the war, we hoped that all of our families would survive the war somehow. But there was no air raid. The Polish air force was no match for the might of the German air force, which the Nazis had been building up since 1933.

1

The German "day of infamy" came during the night of November 9-10, 1938, when all Jewish synagogues in Germany were burned and Jewish-owned shops smashed. Called *Kristallnacht*, or "Night of Broken Glass," this act by Hitler's stormtroopers was in retaliation for the assassination of a German official by a Jewish boy who was protesting the harsh way his family was being treated.

In front of the burning synagogue in my city, my father made the prediction that in a few years many more ruins would surround this ravaged temple. How right he was.

Later at home he showed me, with the help of a globe, that Germany could not win this war. He said, "Look at France and England with all of their colonial resources, and far to the west, the United States. We will not win this war."

I was fourteen years old at the beginning of the war, when I made the secret wish to become a prisoner of war (POW) in North America if the war lasted long enough for me to become of age to be drafted. Since we were involved with Great Britain, my hope was to end up in Canada. But as it turned out, I was even luckier.

Chapter One

"Heil Hitler, You Fat Swine!"

As a boy, my first lesson in keeping my mouth shut about Adolf Hitler took place when I was in the third grade. I scared my teacher when, in front of the whole class, I said the Latin phrase, *Salutem hitlero to porcus crassus!* In English, it means "Heil Hitler, you fat swine!"

Thank heavens, nothing came of the incident. My teacher found out I had learned the words from an older boy and didn't understand what I had said.

Because I *was* so young when Hitler came to power, I wasn't afraid. My family heard it broadcast on the radio when he became chancellor on January 30, 1933. Later, we saw in a newsreel that a big celebration was held in Berlin. Because Jewish people had already been harassed, they probably weren't too happy. They knew what was going to happen.

My father was very much anti-Nazi. He liked Kaiser Wilhelm II, the last German emperor, and he liked President Hindenburg. He had a picture of Hindenburg with his signature.

My father belonged to an organization similar to the American Legion called *Stahlhelm, Bund der Frontsoldaten,* meaning "Steel Helmet, League of Frontline Soldiers." He had a special uniform that he wore to meetings. But in 1934, one of the Nazi leaders, Heinrich Himmler, took over the organization. My father didn't want anything to do with it after that.

3

My mother was anti-Nazi, too. Everyone had to fly the Nazi flag on national holidays, such as Hitler's birthday, April 20, and November 9. This day was when sixteen of Hitler's co-conspirators were killed in 1923 during what was known as the Beer Hall *Putsch* (revolution). It was Hitler's first attempt to start a Nazi revolution. Whenever the flag had to be flown, my mother would say, "We have to put the *lappen* (rag) out today." You never knew if the Gestapo was watching you.

At first, we flew the old German flag of black, white, and red. This was in the early 1930s. Then the old flag was outlawed and we had to fly the new flag, which was red with a large black swastika on it.

My parents, my sister, and I lived on a big square right in the middle of Stettin, where there were five-story apartment buildings. When we met someone, we would say, "Heil Hitler." If we knew the other person was anti-Nazi—as we were—we didn't say it, but we had to be very careful because we could have been denounced. One little thing and you were in jail. We had a saying: *Der größte Lump in Diesem Land ist und Bleibt der Denunziat*, meaning "The biggest scoundrel in the world is someone who denounces you."

My family in Stettin, Germany, in 1927, before the rise of Nazism. From left to right are my mother, Elisabeth; me; my father, Dr. Ernst Floeter; and my sister, Gisela. I was two years old.

I had this one good friend who said "Heil Hitler" to his mother and when he went to bed at night. I don't know if he really believed in Nazism or if he was just being extra careful. The Jewish people in Stettin all wore the required yellow stars. In November of 1938—during *Kristallnacht*—the windows of two Jewish shoe stores in my neighborhood were smashed, with shoes lying everywhere. That was a revelation to me.

In February of 1940, 1,300 Jews living in Stettin were collected and sent to Lublin, Poland, where they either died of starvation or ended up in concentration camps. They were taken from Stettin in the middle of the night. We couldn't see it, but we could hear it. Gypsies and a black family vanished overnight, too.

Two Jewish classmates of mine made it out of Germany to Tel Aviv. They left with their families in a big van with the words "Tel Aviv" painted on it. Most Jews had no money to get out and, besides, no country wanted them.

Signs of the coming war began early in 1939, when butter and coffee were rationed and sometimes hard to get at all. Clandestine ammunition factories appeared in the woods. The newest German airplanes, fighters, and bombers were kept out of sight.

When the war broke out in September, Germans were required to clean out the attics in their apartment buildings. This was a precaution because of fire danger from the bombings. It didn't help much; the buildings went down regardless.

In Stettin, every block had air raid sirens; they had a hellish tone. The sirens were finally synchronized around 1940. Then they wailed in unison all over the city. We experienced the first air raid by the RAF (Royal Air Force) in September 1941 with the bombing of an oil refinery north of us. The Nazis lit big pots of some chemical so our whole town would be foggy. They did this so the airmen couldn't see what was going on. I think the airmen knew more about what was going on than we realized.

Walking through the city on moonless nights, you could see nothing except the luminescent buttons people wore on their coats. There were no streetlights, and the headlights on the few cars had been restricted to a narrow slit.

Every neighborhood had a *blockleiter* (block leader) who was responsible for making sure you obeyed the air raid rules. They kept

5

an eye on everything you did, just like Big Brother in George Orwell's book, *Nineteen Eighty-Four*. All of our windows had to be covered with rolls of dark paper. Heaven forbid if you turned on a light when your window was not covered with this paper. People on the street would get mad and holler *Licht aus!* at you. This meant "Lights out!" It was forbidden even to light a match outside at night because an enemy plane could see light from far away.

In our second-floor apartment, my father said we were safe. We put our clothes next to our beds at night so we could find them fast when the sirens went off. We had to get up and go down into the cellar. Every apartment building had one. I put up signs in the cellar of our building. I remember one was: "Quietness is the first order of civilization." I thought the signs would help people stay calm.

We weren't afraid of the bombing and sometimes went outside; we didn't know any better. I could hear a whistling sound whenever a bomb went over our heads. Funny things happened when bombs hit close by. In a neighboring woman's apartment, a Chinese vase was found standing undamaged while everything around it was ruined. All of the windows in an apartment building shattered, and several locked doors sprang open. But no one I knew was killed.

On April 20, 1943, part of Germany's anti-aircraft cannon supply was taken to Berlin. It was Hitler's fifty-third birthday and a severe bombing raid was anticipated. Instead, British bombers came to Stettin and smashed the southern part of the city. The sun was low and obliterated by smoke. It was like a curtain had come down.

Afterwards, my friends and I dug up long bombs and went up on the rooftops to collect shrapnel. I collected a whole box. Finding bomb shrapnel with an English inscription was considered a real "first prize." It was an interesting time for a boy.

Chapter Two

They Never Talked About It

In spite of all the happenings, my family made the best out of life. As the saying went, "Enjoy the war; the peace will be terrible."

My father was a dentist, and one of his patients had a farm out in the country. My mother and I went there by railway once in a while to get some extra foodstuffs to enrich our table. People had to have such connections to make life more enjoyable. We were able to get wine, chocolate, coffee, soap, and clothing from several sources my father had. He paid with cash, but some people had to barter for the things they needed.

One day my father received a very nice briefcase through the black market. It could have been a family heirloom for us. But the next day he got a call from the police to return it immediately because it was made from stolen leather. So my mother took it back, but not before she poured chloroform in it to make it smelly for a long time.

In 1938, the Nazis held elections asking Germans and Austrians if they were for or against the annexation of Austria. When my father was late in going to vote, two men came to our apartment and took him down to the polls. The German vote was 99 percent "yes." It was either real—or rigged.

I was supposed to join Hitler Youth when I was fourteen, but my town was more liberal than most and didn't enforce the requirement. None of my friends belonged. Even our principal, Karl Schumacher, wanted nothing to do with the Nazi Party. Quite often he would come into our classroom hollering about the Nazis. Once, somebody reported him for some minor political sin for which he had to appear at a political party office.

Sometimes after school a group of us went to a pastry shop for some ice cream. One day a friend of mine put some ice cream on his spoon and flipped it towards a portrait of Hitler. It landed right on his face. We were lucky that no party person was present. The consequences would have been very bad for all of us, and maybe for our parents, too.

There was a concentration camp in my hometown. After Hitler came to power in 1933, a camp was set up in Stettin for people suspected of opposing the Nazi Party. I didn't know about it at the time. If my parents or their friends knew, they never talked about it. If you said anything bad about the Nazis to the wrong person, your life was done. You were either killed or sent to a concentration camp. So you kept your mouth shut.

Every night when atmospheric conditions were good, we listened on our shortwave radio to the BBC's (British Broadcasting Corporation) German-language newscasts from London. The programs came on every hour on the hour and were fifteen or twenty minutes long. First you would hear "dah-dah-dah-DAAAH!" These were the first four notes of Beethoven's *Fifth Symphony*—and the same sounds as the letter "V" in Morse code. The British had adopted the "V" as their victory symbol.

The broadcasts commented on Hitler's speeches and gave anti-Nazi remarks. They told about the Allied bombings, which weren't mentioned in German newspapers. If the only news you got was from German newspapers and the newsreels, you didn't know what was really going on.

Listening to London was a very risky business. If we would have told someone the next day what we had heard on the BBC and this person would have notified the Gestapo, our lives would have been done. Undermining morale was considered even more criminal than murder. Many German heads rolled because of some words that should not have been spoken.

Sometimes the police would go to homes, ring the doorbell, and head straight for the radio to see what station it was set at. We always

changed the setting after listening to the BBC; it was never more than one inch from the *Deutschland* (Germany) station.
Even the churches were affected by the Nazi government. Our Lutheran pastor was a good man, but he followed the Nazi line. We didn't know if he really believed in it or if he was just going along. The clergy in Germany were like civil servants; their wages came from the church taxes everyone had to pay.
I was six years old when I was baptized. When I turned sixteen, I was confirmed, which meant I was then considered an adult. Confirmations were very festive affairs, similar to a bar mitzvah, with gifts and music. The fathers came to church in top hats, and there were special places for the parents to sit. At the church, it was very solemn with the playing of Schubert's *Unfinished Symphony*. Now, every time I hear it, I am reminded of my confirmation. Afterwards, friends and relatives came to our house for cake and coffee. We had connections with a restaurant owner and were able to get a nice cake from him.

An exciting time was when we watched the famous airship *Hindenburg* fly over Stettin. This was in 1937, shortly before it crashed. It was a magnificent site. It was like a silver dollar coming over the horizon. We waved bedsheets from the rooftop. Later I learned that Joseph Goebbels, Hitler's propaganda minister, had ordered the *Hindenburg* flown over German cities as a publicity stunt to make Hitler more popular.

One of my favorite pastimes as a boy was going to the movies, especially American cowboy movies with my idol, Tom Mix. I also saw Shirley Temple and Charlie Chaplin. I had never met an American; I got my good faith in them from these movies.

My friends and I had to sit through the newsreels before we got to see the featured movie. They showed that Germany was always victorious. We never saw any dead German soldiers or damaged equipment. The ushers wore uniforms and chased us out if we tried to see a movie we weren't supposed to see.

Because my father was a dentist, I grew up with screaming women and screaming children. Every doctor and dentist had his office in his home. My father's practice was in our second-floor apartment, where he did all of the oral surgical procedures known at the time. Sometimes my mother would help him in the middle of the night when there was an emergency. An anesthetic was used only for extractions or something really serious. I never heard a man cry; maybe the men thought they were too macho.

All of the businesses in Germany were supposed to have a picture of Hitler on the wall. My father had one, but he got disgusted with it and took it down. The walls in my bedroom were covered with all kinds of pictures, and I had one of Hitler. Once I took my BB gun and shot a hole through it. Later, I took it down and threw it away. I also remember that jokes about Hitler and his Nazi cronies were popular.

Stettin was a pleasant city to grow up in, with lots of woods and lakes around. I had a terrific childhood. When I was fourteen, I bought a bicycle for forty-five reichsmarks and rode it to school, took it on nice trips with my buddies, and even peddled it down the long corridor in our apartment house. My friends and I would also play Indians and cowboys, which we had learned from the American movies. We had tomahawks and headdresses and cap guns. We never played soldier; it wasn't popular then.

I had great parents who took good care of my sister and me. We would play cards and have parties. My father loved nature and we would go on hikes. He was also softhearted and never really punished me. I remember that I made him teary-eyed one Christmas when I said that I didn't get what I had wanted.

My mother was a housewife. She was stricter than my father and kept a switch on top of the kitchen cupboard and would hit me on the back of my legs whenever I misbehaved. But she also had a good sense of humor and liked to have fun. One year, on April Fool's Day, she played a prank on the dentist in the apartment building next to ours. He was a Nazi, and so of course she didn't like him. She called him on the phone, pretending to be the secretary to the governor of our province of Pomerania. She told the dentist that the governor wanted his presence in one hour. He asked her if he should wear his uniform. She replied, "Yes; that would be appropriate." A little while later, we could see him out of our window, strutting like a peacock toward the governor's office. He had no way of knowing that it was my mother who had called him. You couldn't get away with such a thing these days.

We traveled every summer until 1939, when the war started. We went to the Baltic Sea frequently and took steamboat rides. It was very interesting to see the harbors and side rivers. We also hiked in the forests and mountains around our province. We had beautiful woods and there were restaurants where old sawmills used to be.

One time we came across a little restaurant in the woods that sold beer, coffee, and cake, with tables outside and a band playing. It was owned by a retired forest ranger. I thought, "That's what I want to be when I grow up—a retired forest ranger!"

*This photo of me in my sailor suit was taken
in 1933, when I was eight years old.*

We took the train on our vacations until my father bought a car in 1936; then we drove. I remember we went to Silesia and to the Sudetenland the year after it became German. One could get better food in newly annexed areas—cream for coffee, coffee, eggs, butter, and cake.

When the war came in 1939, there was no more driving. Only special people, like those in the military, had permission to drive a car, so my father sold ours. You couldn't get gas anyway. People began to take the trains more and use horse-drawn vehicles.

Every year I got sick. My mother would say, "Your eyes are glassy." I had every illness as a child except diphtheria—bronchitis, chicken pox, measles, mumps, pneumonia, sometimes double pneumonia, and scarlet fever.

My mother gave me a harmonica in 1936 during a time when I was sick in bed. I learned how to play and she was very pleased. The first song I played was the traditional German miner's song, *Deutsch ist Die Saar*. I still play the harmonica to this day.

Because I was sick so much, I missed a lot of school and was getting behind in my lessons. Because of this, my parents began sending me to a private school when I was eleven. The principal there was very nice to me.

In the public school, you had to say "Heil Hitler" every morning when you came in. It was also common for students to get slapped in the face or hit with a bamboo stick. I was slapped several times and got welts on my back from the stick, usually for not knowing the correct answers.

It was different in private school. I could crow like a rooster, and I did this once in geography class when the teacher's back was turned. He didn't know who did it and asked us who it was. No one said anything. Then, when he said he would keep the whole class after school, I admitted it. He didn't punish me, but as I was walking home, he said, "I never would have thought that you would do such a thing."

When Hitler took power, Germans living in countries such as Brazil and Canada began returning to Germany. They believed that "the führer is calling." I thought, "You idiots!" A lot of them settled in Stettin because we were a major port on the Baltic. Their children were some of my classmates.

My favorite subject was geography and I liked to read. But I had no plan for my life because I knew I would become a soldier. Under Hitler's regime, you had to obey the law. When you became of age, you were drafted. It wasn't voluntary.

Chapter Three

Blood and Honor

The Nazis required German boys who reached the age of ten to spend four years in *Deutsches Jungvolk* (German Youth). It was not much fun to be part of it. So, whenever it was possible, I played hooky on Saturdays and spent the time with my parents and sister on nature outings in our beautiful countryside.

One good thing about it was that we were not indoctrinated in Nazi politics like the *Jungvolks* in other cities. We were treated like soldiers in boot camp, with marching, drilling, and singing on Wednesday and Saturday afternoons. When we marched, we always sang traditional German songs or contemporary Nazi songs. In the front of our column was the Nazi flag, which had to be saluted by every citizen who passed us on the street.

We also had to learn the Hitler Youth anthem, "A Young Person Sent Up for the Flag," which we sang on special occasions. We would take three steps, then sing that the Nazi flag is more important than a child's life; that it is "sweet and glorious to die for one's fatherland." It was crazy to have children as young as ten singing such stuff.

In 1942, when I was sixteen, the local officials of Hitler Youth issued a decree ordering all German boys within a certain age range to report to a sports field on a certain day. Because I had not joined Hitler Youth at fourteen, I did not belong to any of the units, like Motor, Air Force, Navy, or Signal Corps. But I had to go. Noncompliance would have resulted in punishment.

I joined the Motor Unit. They took me in and for the next month I went to their meetings twice a week. My uniform consisted of black shorts, a yellow shirt, and a special belt and belt buckle. I was given a knife with the words "Blood and Honor" inscribed on the blade. About the only thing we used it for was cutting our food.

The meetings were a pure waste of time. Nothing interesting went on. The only thing we had to endure was being shouted at by our "juvenile" superior, who was only two years older than I was. Then one day two men arrived in a motorboat to talk to us about how motors run. Finally, something interesting!

Although Hitler Youth was supposed to be a political group, more or less, nothing political was said. We heard some informative talks, drank our beers, and tried to have a good time. It could have been the Salvation Army.

One day a friend of my father's who was a high-ranking officer in the German Army urged me to volunteer for the German Army. He said young men in my birth year of 1925 were going to be drafted into the Weapons SS (*Schutzstaffel*). This was the very last thing I wanted to have happen to me. I knew these fellows were a bad bunch; my folks considered them our enemies.

To avoid that fate, I put in my application for the army's Signal Corps and soon received a letter that I had been accepted. The unit was close to my hometown, so it would be easy for my parents to visit me. Then I waited.

When 1943 came and there was no sign of the war ending, not even after the disastrous Battle of Stalingrad, I knew my time to be drafted would come sometime that year. I was still attending school, which did keep me out of the army for six months, but in May I received my draft notice for the *Reichsarbeitsdienst* (Reich Labor Service).

This program was similar to the Civilian Conservation Corps in America, except it was compulsory. Every German boy and girl who reached the age of eighteen had to participate. And while the purpose was to help reduce unemployment and build up Germany's infrastructure, the Nazis also used it as a way to get young men ready to serve in the German Army.

I was sent to a camp just south of Stettin, close to the Oder River. Most of the leaders at the camp were uneducated bullies who enjoyed their status. During the three months I was there, I spent more than a month in sick bay with bronchitis and persistent fevers that would not go down, mostly because of the pillow fights in my ward.

My work at the camp consisted primarily of making bricks. The other fellows and I had to bicycle every day to an embankment north of Stettin, about a one-and-a-half hour ride, to make the bricks. Another job I had was peeling potatoes.

Each one of us there had a spade; it was our symbol. We had to do drills with the spades just like soldiers do with their rifles. The spades had to be clean and shiny all of the time. Every night an officer checked them, and if one was dirty he would throw it off the rack. Water would then be poured all over the floor, and we had two hours to mop it up. If it wasn't cleaned up in that time, we had to get out of bed in our nightgowns in the middle of the night and march outside.

I was thankful that on August 11, I became a free man again—that is, until the postman (who was now a lady) presented me with an order to report on August 20 for induction into the German Army. Then, just two days before I had to report, I got sick again and my father had to call the military hospital. My guardian angel was watching out for me! Since I wasn't able to follow the orders, I had more free time until the army wanted me again on September 30. If the army had known that such a "great" soldier was coming into its ranks, it would have excused me.

Chapter Four

Praying for Deliverance

I left home with a funny feeling on a dreary morning. After saying goodbye to my sad-looking parents, I walked to a sports field where quite a big group had assembled. The officers there checked us to make sure we were the right fellows, then everyone got on a train.

We ended up in Rostock, about 250 kilometers northwest of Stettin. Here we were introduced to Prussian discipline—making our bed, shining our shoes, keeping our locker neat—if we didn't already know how to do these things. If I had known that in a year I would be picking cotton in New Mexico, I would have been happy.

After a few days in Rostock, we were transferred to an Infantry Signal Corps Training Unit in Danzig, now Gdansk, Poland. We learned Morse code, telephone, and radio in an old red brick building called the Kaserne. Outside were horse stables and a large drilling area, with a high wall around the perimeter.

About fifteen privates shared a room, plus a corporal. My room was number seventeen. The mattresses on the beds were made of old straw and must have been infested because bite marks appeared all over my legs. They looked pretty bad, which scared my sergeant, but the marks went away on their own.

We drilled every Monday from six in the morning to twelve noon. I had been the tallest student in my class at school and was the fourth tallest soldier here out of about 100. We always marched three across, so my place was in the second row.

Here it was discovered that I needed to wear glasses. We had to shoot at a target on a sandbag and I couldn't see it. I was given an eye exam and ended up with two pairs of glasses, one regular pair and another to fit inside my gas mask. That night I looked up . . . I could see stars!

Unteroffizier Baudi, our drill sergeant in Danzig, had a difficult time with me because I was a stupid soldier. Except at the shooting range, I made lots of mistakes—like stumbling in parade formations and not being able to estimate distances. He gave me a hard time whenever the opportunity arose, and so I hated him and he hated me. One time he said to me, "You're a public nuisance." On the other hand, our commanding officer, *Oberleutnant* Mueller, by profession a teacher, was good-natured.

There was no political indoctrination at boot camp whatsoever. It was always "Good morning, soldier" and "Good evening, soldier," never "Heil Hitler." That was nice.

A master sergeant, whose name I forget but whom we called the "mother" of our company, always carried his famous black book that contained all of our "sins" from the past week. When Saturday came for the weekend formations, he would read the names of all those who did something wrong. Most of the time, mine was among them. This meant I had to report to the stables for cleaning the stalls or operate a big machine and cut straw for two hours. The officers were very inventive in their punishments.

All of it was quite tiresome and how often I had wished to get sick and spend time in sick bay. But in the long run, it was much better to stay healthy and endure bad times. In the army you are never alone, unless you are in one location where even a king is alone. There, I must have done some praying for deliverance and a better future.

Whenever privates wore their caps, they were required to give a military salute to officers. It was only when they didn't have on a cap that they had to raise their arms and say "Heil Hitler." One time I saluted Baudi with "Heil Hitler." He said to me, "Don't you know you have your cap on?" But in the end, doing stupid things like that saved my life.

In December, we went on a maneuver to Marienburg, south of

Danzig. Today it is called Malbork. Those were dreadful days. I lost my glasses and tore a hook off my uniform, which was surely a crime as my dear sergeant saw it. He found delight in it by giving me his filthy hat to wash and his shoes to clean and by ordering me to make a fire in his stove with peat.

This photo of me as Private Floeter was taken when I was at boot camp in Danzig, Germany, in the spring of 1944. I was eighteen years old.

After a few weeks into our training, we were allowed to go into the city on weekends, but not before we proved that we could salute correctly. We were under orders to salute all NCOs (noncommissioned officers) and, for sure, all officers. We were all quite scared about doing it right, so we saluted even nonmilitary men as long as they wore any kind of uniform.

On Christmas Eve, we had a company party. I only remember a speech by an officer—not from our unit—who made derogatory remarks about the Christ Child and the meaning of Christmas and other religious institutions. After a while, we sneaked out of the room and celebrated Christmas with our own small tree.

Despite some reluctance from Baudi, I got a pass for three days to meet with my parents in Zoppot. There, one could get restaurant meals, which were no longer available in the "old reich." For my father, it was a reunion. He had spent his basic training before World War I in Danzig, too, in almost the same brick barracks as his son. Later on, he was a field dentist in France during that war, 1914-1918.

In January 1944, our whole unit went to Thorn—now Torun, Poland—for special training with live ammunition and hand grenades. Here, for a change, everything went rather well and that made Baudi happy.

One incident did occur with the hand grenade exercise. We had to throw the grenades at these so-called "cardboard comrades" that appeared out of the ground. The heads, which looked British, were small and hard to see. Well, I had a difficult time and our commanding officer, Mueller, predicted that I would be the first one to get killed when it came to the real thing. As it turns out, I may be the only survivor of them all.

Baudi continued to be happy with me until I received a telegram from my parents. It urged me to come home because Stettin had been bombed and our apartment was heavily damaged. When this happened, a soldier could get special permission to go home. Baudi did not like this one bit—that I, of all the others, could go home. Well, he let me feel that one, too. When it came to writing my request for the leave, I had to write it over and over. He found something wrong with my writing every time. Finally, another sergeant told him to "stop this nonsense" and let me go.

I caught the train at the station just in time and arrived in Stettin the next day. The uniform I wore was not the best, especially my boots, which looked like little barges. I think I got some better ones later on.

The large, five-story apartment building my parents lived in was located in the middle of the city. The damage had been done by air pressure from bombs that had destroyed the adjacent buildings. Because my father's office had suffered severe damage, he had to practice at the home of a colleague. I spent several days at home while my unit had to march fifty miles in Thorn.

One day I accompanied my mother downtown, where she threw a paper bag into some ruins. She wouldn't tell me what the bag contained. Later that day she revealed the secret. In the cellar of our apartment house, local officials had filled a big storage room with food, including marmalade, to supply the citizens in case the city came under siege. The wife of our landlord told my mother about this cache, and both went down into the cellar and took a tin can of marmalade. Apparently my mother realized later that she had better not get caught with it. As it turned out, it never came to a siege and all of the goodies were destroyed by fire.

As the good Lord had wanted, I got sick while I was home. I had to travel by train to the next available hospital, in Gollnow, which was not too far away. Here I spent fifteen days with a bunch of nice comrades. Oh, they could tell some stories! We all smoked majorca, a very coarse tobacco. It didn't taste too bad . . . but the smell! It went right into the walls and our clothing. But as a smoker, I welcomed anything.

After I was discharged from the hospital, I received two weeks of leave before returning to my unit in Danzig. Oh, the officers were happy to see me now . . . not that they missed me . . . absolutely not. But just a day earlier, the general had come for review, and they were sure I would have spoiled the whole business if I had been present. What luck for all of us! By now, I was certain there was a purpose to the happenings in my life.

The very next day, all of the soldiers who were going into action received two weeks' leave. They told me I wouldn't get it—that I had just had mine. But one officer took pity on me and I was given leave, too. I went back to Stettin for fourteen quiet days, visiting friends all around and catching up on the newest movies. Time to say *auf wiedersehen* (goodbye) came too fast.

Chapter Five

They Would Not See the
End of the War

When my fellow soldiers and I returned to Danzig, we were told we would go to Marienburg. These next nineteen days were not pleasant, to say the least. It was bitter cold. Our training consisted of putting telephone cables over trees with our bare hands. That was not for me.

The best thing in that town was the Castle of the Teutonic Order, built in the thirteenth century. It was a beautiful historic monument. Later on, in 1945, it suffered heavy damage. After the war, Marienburg became part of Poland and the castle was restored to its former glory.

Now came the time for good soldiers to be selected for sergeant school. Good fortune was with me again. The suffering I had withstood at the hands of my drill sergeant had a purpose. The guys who had been excellent recruits and had done a splendid job during training were going away to this school.

Three soldiers, including me, were not selected. This was not a surprise as Baudi had said I was the best example of how *not* to do things. I said goodbye to my friends, not knowing then that they would not live to see the last days of the war, when we were fighting against the Russians. Privates Arens and Hoeft were the other soldiers who did not qualify for sergeant school.

The three of us boarded a troop train, already filled with soldiers, that was destined initially for Wismar, a small port on the Baltic Sea. On the way we stopped at a camp where we had an inspection of our gear. Thank heavens, the inspecting officer did not look at mine because I had left my glasses in Marienburg. Not having all of your stuff could result in drastic consequences, especially if the missing item, like my glasses, had been issued by the military.

On the train going west, we stopped outside of Stettin. It was April 2. Some of us asked our transport commander if the soldiers whose hometown was Stettin could be let off. After some hesitation, he gave us permission, but with our word of honor that we would return at a given time.

We took off in a hurry and surprised our folks with this unexpected visit of two hours. By this time, the city was pretty much bombed out. All of the big houses downtown had become burned-out shells; fortunately, not our block. I didn't know this would be the last time I would see my hometown for forty-eight years. I would not see my parents again for thirty months. It would be under different circumstances, but at least we would be in good shape.

In Wismar, we all slept on the floor in one big room. Because of the total darkness, we had a hard time not stepping on others when we went to the john in the middle of the night. Lights of any kind were forbidden because an enemy plane might spot us.

Back on the train, we passed through many destroyed cities in the Ruhr Valley, especially Wuppertal. There was not much left of that town.

Slowly it got warmer and we arrived in the town of Baumholder in the state of Palatine. A brand-new division, the 91st Air Landing Division, was just being assembled under the leadership of General Wilhelm Falley. We became part of this division, with Major Sylvester von Saldern-Brallentin as our immediate superior in Grenadier-Regiment 1057. We were still considered infantry.

I had a more pleasant time in Baumholder. The barracks were new and had showers, and the officers tried to treat us fairly because they needed our loyalty in battle. More importantly, I found out that I was not the most stupid soldier in the German Army.

Baumholder in those days was filled with soldiers. Come evening, there was hardly a place to sit in the local restaurant. Here we saluted only the officers as there was no longer a requirement to salute NCOs. By this time there were just too many of them.

Some of the soldiers in our unit were Russians who had volunteered. Most were White Russians from Belarus, a contested area in Eastern Europe taken over by the Russians in 1939 when the war began. Then the Nazis took Belarus in 1941 when they invaded the Soviet Union. I remember when the White Russian soldiers marched, they always sang beautifully. At the end of the war, all of these poor guys were sent back to their homeland and executed immediately.

Because we were an air landing unit, we had exercises with both big and small gliders. We were all quite pessimistic that we could carry out an air landing according to what we were told and then, after a turbulent landing, be fit to fight. I thought, "We'll be dead before we hit the ground."

This dog tag is the only souvenir I have from my German Army days. Worn on a chain around the neck, the dog tag is broken in two if the soldier is killed, with half placed between his teeth and the other half sent to Berlin.

Every day huge numbers of American airplanes crossed the sky, flying eastward. We were ordered to go into the shelters, but often we just hid under our beds. At night, when the air raids sounded, we had a hard time finding our clothing in the pitch darkness.

One time a buddy and I were lucky to escape a terrible disaster. We had to man an anti-aircraft gun, but we weren't sure how to operate the piece. It was a nice day, nothing had happened so far, and so we lay down and, oh my God, fell asleep. Our luck was with us as the wife of an officer—not an officer—came by and woke us.

On Hitler's birthday, April 20, we were told by our major that the entire 91st Division was destined for a war-deciding mission. What it would be, he would not tell us. We were supposed to guess. It could only have meant a landing in England—just when England was filled with armaments ready for the Allies' planned invasion of Europe.

(Hitler's birthday that year was a historic day for me. Until then, I did not have to shave; I just had a little growth on my chin. An officer noticed this and got at me with, *Wie koennen Sie es wagen am Geburtstag unseres Fuhres unrasiert herumzulaufen!* In English: "How dare you to run around on our führer's birthday unshaved!")

The higher command apparently changed its plans because on May 1 we boarded a train and traveled west, passing through Strasbourg and Orléans, France, to Saint-Nazaire, France. The trip took nearly three days. Once in a while the train stopped for nature calls, and at one of these stops someone got hold of French cigarettes. What a Kraut! But they were too strong and some of us got sick.

We put up our camp on the outskirts of Saint-Nazaire. For ten days this camp was our home. The first thing on our agenda was to dig a hole for the latrine with a *DonnerBalken* (thunder beam). One day I found out there was a farm nearby. I went over to try out my French, which I had studied for nearly six years. To my dismay, the only French I could converse with the old woman there was "Ooh la la, ooh la la." The French spoken around Saint-Nazaire was quite different from what I had learned in school.

As usual, I made a bad impression on a young lieutenant because I was "merely a student." This officer gave me an order to get him a container to fetch water in. As a private, I had to obey. I started looking for one and spied a ceramic jug outside in the grass. I looked around to see if anyone saw me and then committed my first crime by stealing the jug.

I didn't realize at the time what a predicament I could have been in if I had been caught. But it didn't make any difference to this lieutenant where I got the jug as long as I brought him something. He had given me his machine pistol, and for that I got chewed out by another superior. Privates were not allowed to carry such a weapon; it was a privilege only for officers.

After ten days in the boondocks, we finally arrived at our destination—the Cotentin Peninsula in Normandy. We arrived there on May 16, somewhere in the countryside. I was assigned to a small unit of telephone operators living in a bunker. They told us an Allied invasion would take place here, but when, that was the big question.

Whenever atmospheric conditions were favorable for a landing, we had to be on guard duty an extra two hours to watch the sky for paratroopers. This meant four hours in all and nearly every night. During the day, we worked in low-lying areas, chopping down trees and planting them in upright positions (we called them "Rommel asparagus") to make obstacles for enemy planes.

One night I received an order to go up a hill with a soldier who outranked me and deliver a message to the unit there. Here, again, I got into trouble. It was dark and we lost our way in the underbrush, which had been all burned up. After much delay we found the unit, but not before the burned branches tore our uniforms. I counted thirty little triangles in mine. After that, I had to wear my fatigues.

We, especially me, heard it from our superior. This, too, had a reason. My guardian angel was watching over me again! The regiment's staff company needed another telephone operator, so they happily shipped me out to Saint-Sauveur-le-Vicomte, where the regimental headquarters was located. The major and his staff lived on the estate; the telephone operators, in a bunker in the park. We did our washing and cleaning in a little stream that ran through the park. For our natural business, we grabbed a shovel and went into the woods.

Finally, I could breathe some relief. We had drill here, too, but the big difference was now I did everything right and others made the mistakes. Our job here was to lay telephone cables all over the countryside. We also had guard duty in the park each night for four hours—two hours with a buddy and two hours alone. The park was full of owls, which made the experience a rather eerie one. Each time I was finished with guard duty, I would have to wake up the next fellow, who would swear at me because he didn't want to get up.

In this sector, the French population was treated rather well by the Germans; it always depended on the local German commander. I was getting along better speaking French and found that the French people were very nice to us. They complained more about the British when they dropped their bombs. The French would say, "Tommy boom-boom."

For me, there was not enough to eat—even though we were given extra rations because of our young age. My father had sent me some

25

money, so every night I went to a farm in the village and bought butter, milk, and eggs.

All of this food still was not enough to quell my hunger, so I convinced our supply sergeant to give me a loaf of *Kommisbrot* (coarse rye bread) every other day. That, together with a lot of butter, was just the right thing. We were ordered to boil our milk, which worked out okay as long as we didn't let it stay too long on the fire. One day we received a good supply of beer, *Schnaps*, and French red wine. That night I got drunk, and the next morning a few other guys, besides me, swore never to touch the stuff again.

There was a little cemetery for German soldiers on the grounds of this park. Most of the fallen had died from their own mistakes while on guard duty. Some were killed while rabbit hunting. Others were shot by their own buddies who were trigger-happy and reacted to the slightest noise. Sadly, those bullets hit their mark.

I always thought that the soldiers who were involved in these accidents were probably excellent recruits during their training. But when it came to the real conditions of war, they went to pieces.

Chapter Six

Mortar Shells Straight at Us

Shortly before D-Day, my regiment was sent to Sainte-Mere-Eglise, which earned its fame the night of June 5 when American paratroopers landed in the center of that town. All through the previous night we could hear explosions coming from the coast, not too far away. The Allies were trying to destroy Normandy's coastal defenses.

The next day the weather turned bad, so there was no reason to expect an invasion that night. Our regional commander, Field Marshal Erwin Rommel, went to Berlin to celebrate his wife's birthday.

The supreme commander of the Allied Expeditionary Force, General Dwight D. Eisenhower, had other ideas and started the invasion. It was a memorable day in my life because I had just written a letter to my parents that morning, not knowing it would be the last one for two months.

Since the weather wasn't suitable that night for any enemy action—at least that's what the higher command thought—we had no extra watch duty. It was uneventful until about 10:30, when I awoke from hearing awful noises overhead. I looked out of my tent flap and saw a huge armada of American warplanes crossing the sky, heading eastward. It was rather frightful, as my buddies and I correctly assumed the planes were on a bombing mission.

Even though we were part of the Regimental Staff Company,

nobody knew what in heaven was going on until about midnight, when news finally came through that the nightly waiting was over . . . the predicted invasion had begun.

The next day, June 6, we had to destroy all of our telephone cables. The air was filled with American and British fighter planes, and no soldier on the ground was safe because the fliers attacked anyone they saw.

We were told that Field Marshal Rommel would come with his tanks, but thank heavens that didn't happen. Hitler could not be disturbed, and, besides, he always thought any invasion would take place at the narrowest point in the English Channel—between Calais and Dover. He believed *this* invasion was a diversion.

From the first hour on, the Allied air forces held superior. Not one German plane was in sight. We common soldiers had no idea what was going on at Omaha Beach and what the American landing force had to suffer until they were able to clear the beachhead. The casualties on both sides were tremendous. Our division commander, General Wilhelm Falley, was killed, together with a major, before he could give any orders to his staff. During the night of June 6, we were told to watch the sky for additional paratroopers, but that part of the invasion was over.

On the morning of June 8, we packed up our stuff onto two-wheelers and moved toward the American lines. There was no direct front; the American, British, and Canadian troops were scattered all over the countryside.

We were lucky that no airplanes spotted us. We made it safely to our destination, somewhere between Saint-Sauveur-le-Vicomte and the coast. Here I met up again with the young lieutenant who had ordered me to take that ceramic jug. Oh, how friendly he was all of a sudden. He was now afraid he would be shot from behind if he continued with his nasty disposition. All of our superiors here were humane and took good care of us—what a difference from those in basic training.

We camped in a small stone hut and were issued live ammunition, about ninety rounds, and some hand grenades. The rifle I was given, a Karabiner 98k, was the weapon most German soldiers carried. But mine didn't work properly because it had been put together from two rifles. Thank God I never came into a situation where I had to use it. I think if I had had to shoot at any Americans, I would have aimed over their heads. American soldiers impressed me with their kind hearts and sense of fairness; I had good faith in them.

The food distributed included the so-called "iron ration," a can of sausage. This was a kind of emergency ration in case nothing else was available. At one point, I found a nicely wrapped candy bar lying on the ground—at least that's what I thought it was. I was always after sweets. As a boy, I would spend my whole allowance on candy. Well, I took one bite and had to spit it out. It tasted like grease—nothing like what I had hoped for. I never learned what it really was. Another time, someone gave me an American cigarette, a Philip Morris. It was *some* smoke. It acted like a drug compared to German cigarettes.

During the evening of June 8, we were told the Americans would attack the next morning. We were ordered to dig in on a small hill; this would be the first foxhole of many during the next nine days. It was hard digging with our small shovels because there were so many stones, but we finally succeeded in digging holes big enough for two. They weren't very deep, but with an earthen wall all around, we felt pretty safe. Early in the morning our task was done and we fell asleep.

After only a few hours, we had to get up and frisk five American prisoners of war. They were tall fellows with blackened faces, and afraid. They had been wounded, some severely. I felt sorry for them and hoped they would get good care very fast. We had to take away their money—bills with pictures of Hitler, Mussolini, and Hirohito with nooses around their necks—and any sharp instruments. They also had some comic books with rather corny jokes. I hope they all made it back after the war.

We had just finished with the Americans when mortar shells started coming straight at us. That made all of us run to our foxholes. I didn't have time to retrieve my helmet. I had on just my field cap, which didn't make me feel very secure, sitting there in our shallow foxhole with mortars exploding close by. It looked and sounded like a sniper was taking aim at our location. It was a frightful baptism by fire.

My buddy was Werner Mueller from Coburg. He was not tall, so he had better protection than I did. After a long time—at least it seemed so—there was a pause in the mortar fire. Looking out, we saw German soldiers retreating in a hurry. Well, we jumped out, too.

Grabbing a helmet from a dead German sergeant, I followed the crowd. Everyone was running like the devil was after them, throwing away their equipment to lighten their loads.

I kept my stuff, and all of a sudden I realized I was among strange soldiers. I had no idea where I was. The best thing in this situation was to go back where I came from, or so I thought. It was a beautiful morning, the birds were singing—but in the distance I could hear the war going on.

I finally arrived where I had started from and gathered up all of our food supplies and, most importantly, my helmet. (The helmet I had found had a loose rivet and flopped on my head.) The area was completely deserted and peaceful until a German car came by with some officers who asked what I was doing there. I told them, and they said I could load up with bread and sausage at the next stop. That was funny, I thought. Where on earth would the "next stop" be?

The best thing for me to do was to start walking. Going through some woods nearby, I came to a farm and look what was there . . . my outfit! What luck! Just then an American tank passed by. Because of this, we had an all-alert for the night—when my guardian angel was with me again. The radio operator from our unit was wounded and a replacement was needed. I got the job, and from then on we were one team with *Unteroffizier* Pfeiffer. He was a good-natured fellow and we got along nicely.

During that first night nothing was seen again of the American tank. We retreated the next day, ending up in a pasture in the company of a herd of cows that must have been in pain. The French farmer was not to be seen, and these cows were in desperate need of being milked. Some fellows tried their luck, but with no success. After two days, the cows were gone.

Radio communication was forbidden because our troops were too close. To top it off, the Americans were not too far away either. From then on we spent our days in one foxhole, having nothing to do. One good thing was that I didn't have to carry the heavy radio. Pfeiffer had it put in the ambulance. This wasn't quite kosher, but . . . . Later on, the radio would be blown up.

Somewhere I had learned that most French farmers made their own cider, hard and sweet. On June 10 I found a terrific source. After collecting canteens, I made my way to a farm that wasn't too far away. Nobody was around and in the barn were two big barrels of this good stuff. I had to consume quite a bit before I noticed some results from the alcohol. Here I was, lying down and enjoying the cider, while American planes strafed the countryside. Then I loaded up and returned with my treasure. I had just made it back to my unit when mortar fire started again.

Chapter Seven

"The Amis Are Here!"

From the sound of the constant shelling, we knew the Americans were nearby. During the noon hour the firing ceased, so we had time to do our business while staying close to our havens. Maybe the Americans used this time for their own relief. Over our heads we heard big grenades traveling into the hinterland. These were not of concern to us. We were worried about the small ones that we had to endure nearly all day long. These mortars hit between the several foxholes. During the night, both sides went to sleep until eight in the morning.

On June 11, after sitting comfortably in our hole during a lull, I heard something that sounded like an old man, with a low moaning voice, shuffling through the grass. Immediately I felt as though I had been hit in the back by something. It didn't seem like much. I lifted up and right then I felt something hot under my seat. Reaching down, I found a rather large piece of shrapnel. I poked my hand into my coat and discovered that I must be bleeding somewhere because my hand was all bloody.

Although the wound proved to be superficial, my comrade Pfeiffer, in a near panic, alerted the medic. At the first good moment, I crawled over to the medic, who bandaged my wound with an American dressing and wound powder, which helped it to heal very fast. The bandage had a strap that went around my shoulder. It was quite uncomfortable, and later on I cut it off and threw the whole thing away.

To my astonishment, I learned the medic had just returned from the American lines under the protection of the Red Cross. Earlier, a German officer had asked me what the Red Cross sign looked like; he didn't know it was an international symbol. He had shot at an American vehicle bearing a blue star, later worrying that it may have been a Red Cross sign. I told him he hadn't committed a crime, which made him very happy. What a dummy!

The following night I had to carry our heavy radio—about ninety pounds—on my back when we retreated to another location, this time a deserted French farmhouse. Here, too, I found the cider barrels. Our unit was still getting food, mostly very early in the morning when the chuck wagon made it through. This was like a chimney stove on wheels. We always got a good-tasting goulash with beans and meat in it—very hearty, a good soldier meal.

The next morning, not bothered by enemy fire, we arrived at a large red brick building that looked like a monastery. As we approached from one side, French fellows ran out the opposite side, probably to the Americans to tell them of our whereabouts. We had interrupted their dinner plans for we found hanging in the huge fireplace a big kettle with a whole pig's head, ready to be eaten. What a feast for a change! Except for an invalid old man lying in bed, no one was to be found.

I set my radio in one corner of the grounds and, by golly, received my first message in Morse code. I wish I could remember what that message was. With enemy fire all around, I soon had to move into a barn. It got a bit harrowing in there, too. One time I walked outside, and right then a mortar round hit the barn just where I had been standing a moment earlier.

Behind the main house was a strawberry patch. The berries weren't quite ripe, but nevertheless we ate them. We were all hungry for fruit of some kind, ripe or not. I dug my foxhole next to the berry patch, where the ground was ideal for digging. As soon as I had finished laying some boards over my "country home," American mortars zeroed in, hitting the main house. Thanks to those boards, I was saved from falling bricks and roof tiles.

I sat in my foxhole, waiting for things to come—which appeared before long in the form of an American unit. One of our soldiers had retreated without notifying the regimental staff, and here through the breach the Americans came. We all ran for our lives. We scurried down a slope, trying not to get hit by tracer bullets, which made quite a "Fourth of July" effect over our heads. I dove behind a small hedge, hoping for some cover. Beside me were crates filled with German *Panzerfaust* (bazookas) with an inscription saying they were "not to fall into enemy hands."

A sergeant nearby got hit in the belly. That scared me as that was one spot where I did not want to be wounded. By this time it was completely dark; no moonlight or stars. While lying behind that hedge, I got hit in the throat. "This is the end for me," I thought. I felt around the spot, but I couldn't find a hole or anything; there was just a bit of wetness. I was *so* relieved and said to myself, "I must have made it!"

Once I realized I was okay, I knew I had better get out of there. I started to run down the left side of the slope. I was all alone, with no one in sight. All of a sudden someone grabbed me by the collar and turned me to the right. I thought my guardian angel must have been that person; there is no other explanation. Well, I knew I had better take the hint. I ran down the right side of the slope . . . and right into my friends.

We were all fed up with the mortar fire and decided to get away as quickly as possible. We kept away from the road by climbing over fences and through farms until we came to the outskirts of Saint-Sauveur-le-Vicomte, right back to where we had started some days earlier.

Our commander, Major von Saldern-Brallentin, was getting our unit together, with lost soldiers from other branches joining us. Then we were what was called a *Kampftruppe*, a "strike force" made from various units. We spent that night without sleeping. The next morning, to everyone's delight, we marched eastward to get away from it all.

But it was not to be. After only a few miles, we were ordered to take cover and wait. I heard from one of the men in our unit that the Telephone Unit, Second Company, had been wiped out. No survivors. And that was the company I had belonged to before I was assigned to the Staff Company.

It wasn't long before we found ourselves back in the chaos, back in Saint-Sauveur-le-Vicomte, to defend the town. I was milling about the downtown area when I got the order to dig in on the side of a hill and set up my radio there. The view from the hill became quite interesting as American Mustangs started to bomb the town. It was like having the best seat in the theater.

I checked my rifle, which I had not had to use so far. I hoped it would stay that way. I didn't want to kill any Americans who had come to rid us of the Nazis. My rifle wouldn't have worked anyway; the ejector was broken. I did find a Luger pistol, so I had something to defend myself with besides my five grenades.

That night I moved with a large group of other soldiers into a nearby farm built in a "U" shape. We occupied the middle part. I had left behind my gas mask, which had become quite a nuisance. Most soldiers had already done that. Some of them kept the container to put food in, which was much more important than the gas mask. I had made up my mind that if I had to throw away my gear, I would keep the mess kit and spoon.

Someone had discovered a telephone cable on the farm, and an order was given asking for volunteers to find the source. I had nothing else to do and it sounded interesting, so I volunteered. My comrades and I followed the cable for many miles into the country until we came to the road to Cherbourg. One of us suggested we stop right there since the Americans were supposed to be beyond the railroad tracks. We connected our phone to the line to report back, but we were ordered to proceed. This we did not do; instead, we turned right around.

While we were gone, all of the remaining soldiers had been ordered to get out and fight nearby. In the meantime, American airplanes were dropping leaflets in Polish and German, urging Poles in German uniforms to surrender. I didn't know of any Polish soldiers in our unit, only Russians.

After midnight we made it back to the farm, sacked down, and went to sleep. We didn't get much sleep because at dawn we were awakened by gunfire. The Americans were occupying a nearby hill and shooting directly into the barnyard. Our major called out that we should all meet, and then we ran for our lives, once again. I think from then on the major made his own decisions more than ever before. With General Falley gone, there didn't appear to be any communication from higher up, no strategic plan for retreat.

What else does the German Army do? It marches, and that's

what we did. All over the place we saw destruction: dead horses and smashed wagons. Fortunately, I didn't see any dead GIs because we were behind the main action. We stopped along the road to La Haye du Puits and dug another foxhole, only to find the Americans had crawled over a hill just one mile away. Off we went very fast until we were far enough away to camp for the night.

The next morning we approached a checkpoint, but the military police would not let us through. We had to turn back. If he *had* let us through, the course of events in my life would have changed—and maybe I would not be here today.

The next day, June 16, we had nothing to eat. We came to a farm and, oh, what a surprise! Several milk cans there were full of whipping cream. What a feast again! Forgotten was the class difference. The major borrowed my mess kit and enjoyed it as much as we did.

The following day we were walking through a forest when incoming fire made us run again. The ambulance got hit and that took care of our radio. After running through the woods on the double, we came to a clearing. The shelling was light. I saw a German captain digging his foxhole. When the Americans started to fire fog grenades, I got a bit concerned since my gas mask was gone. We were all shaken up, but not in any real danger, so we decided to camp here. This would be our last night in the German Army.

The weather was perfect during the whole time, not one drop of rain. A rainstorm would have put a damper on all this excitement, as perilous as it was. On the beachhead, it must have been very different.

On June 18, just twelve days after D-Day, we came to an orchard surrounded by hedgerows about five feet thick and eight feet tall. At two o'clock in the afternoon, we paused and rested. I lay under a blooming apple tree and fell asleep. Come nightfall, a buddy woke me and said, "The Amis are here!"

I crawled over to the side along the hedgerow and waited for things to happen. The American soldiers were all around us behind the hedges, shooting over our heads, and calling and shouting. It was quite a show; the whole situation was actually rather funny.

After a while a German officer called to us to shoot back. What a fool. That would have been a suicide maneuver. Then a German soldier stood up, pulled a white towel out of his pack, and started to wave it. Although we were pretty well armed, sixty men and eight officers, this was the best thing he could have done because we were caught like a mouse in a trap.

Out front there was a path through the hedges. A GI came through, pointing his gun at us, and said something like, "Come on, boys." I got up, opened my belt with all of its paraphernalia, and let it drop. I took my rifle and smashed it to the ground. The first thought that hit me was, "Thank God, no more rifle drills!"

Chapter Eight

Crackers with a Splendid Jam

Now I was where I wanted to be . . . almost. After eight months in the German Army, I was happy that episode of my life was over. Now I was afraid of being liberated by our own troops. I did not want to fight for *that* Germany and die for the glory of the Nazis.

The first thing the Americans did was tend to our wounded; then they took care of the rest of us. The eight officers remained behind and I did not see them again.

We sixty men assembled in a long row to be frisked. My friend, Werner Mueller, stood beside me and was approached by a Polish-American who spoke fluent German. He asked him how old he was. When Werner told him, the GI got angry, not at Werner, but at our commander, who must have told him that he didn't have soldiers that young in his group. I was eighteen, and Werner was younger than I was.

When it came to being searched, I had the pleasure of meeting a very nice GI. He took away my diary, knife, scissors, and a metal coin, which he threw on the ground. I must have said something in French because he asked me if I spoke the language. I said "yes" and begged him to pick up the coin and give it back to me because it was a souvenir from Bavaria and a good luck piece, too.

He bent down, picked it up, and put it in my pocket. That was a really nice gesture and it made a big impression on me. We had been told by one of our superiors that the Americans killed their prisoners. I did not believe this.

After this rather pleasant start of our new life, we had to march for a while until we came to a ditch. Then we were ordered to stand still, hold our hands folded on top of our heads, and wait. Behind us were the GIs with their loaded machine pistols. With some apprehension I stood, it seemed, for a very long time until my right hand became completely numb. By squeezing my fingers together, I could manage to keep my hands where they belonged.

Then, because of some movement, my glasses slipped off my nose. I caught them with my mouth. There I was, standing there, not knowing what to do. If I put my glasses on myself, I might be shot. If I let them drop, they might be lost. I started to wiggle them, and, lo and behold, a good soldier came around from behind and put them back on my nose. Right then, I think I felt sure that nothing bad could, or would, happen to us.

We began marching again with our hands on the shoulders of the guy in front of us. We came to a motor pool and began our first ride on an American truck. We passed through Saint-Sauveur-le-Vicomte, where I saw some enormous craters along the road. The famous American war correspondent Ernie Pyle mentioned these in his book, *Brave Men*. The town itself was gutted and full of rubble.

Outside of town, where I had just been two weeks earlier laying telephone cables, we could see how the American Signal Corps had installed their cables—all topsy-turvy, thrown over trees in big bundles. If we would have done it the same way, it would have been considered a crime. We always had to do things according to the book, and, well, who won the war?

Finally we arrived at a "holding pen," which was surrounded by a single strand of wire. Lots of GIs were sitting and sleeping on the outside. By now it was night and probably cold, but in our excitement, we couldn't feel the cold. Here we slept until morning. Since we had had nothing to eat, we were pretty hungry. The Americans were not allowed to give us part of their rations, but they looked away in a casual manner and tossed us some cookies.

We were up on the trucks again, rolling toward the coast. Just before reaching Omaha Beach, we stopped and found out how lucky we were. On this spot, a huge cemetery was going to be built. We were told that if we had been captured just one day earlier, we would have gotten the awful job of collecting dead GIs.

From here we marched for a long time over hills and dunes to an area called Saint-Laurent-sur-Mer. The road had been fortified with steel mesh to make it easier to drive over the sand. A continuous convoy of trucks came toward us, heading inland. I had the thought that if anyone still believed in a German victory after seeing these supplies—and especially when we came over the dunes and saw what was going on at the beachhead with all of the ships and boats in the water—he must be nuts.

It was an awesome sight for our eyes. This was the place where so many American soldiers gave their lives on that famous day, June 6. Now it looked almost peaceful. We were led beyond the beach to a bowl-like earthen structure. The captured German officers occupied one part, the NCOs another, and we, the small fry, had to camp in the middle.

At last we were given some food in the form of C rations. What a delight! Because Nescafé was new to us, we didn't know what to do with it until we got educated and put it in water for a genuine cup of coffee, even a cold one. Everyone received two cans of C rations twice a day. I noticed that some prisoners were going through the line twice. I thought, if they can do that, so can I. I got away with this three times before the guards announced that some of us were double-dipping and would be executed if caught. That stopped my hunger immediately.

That night we *did* feel the cold. Now I regretted that I had lost my field cap when we were "liberated." I cut a piece of material off my pants, placed it on my head, and secured it with a French tricolor pin I had found in Saint-Sauveur-le-Vicomte. My good friend Werner had the fine idea of getting an army blanket by explaining that his kidneys needed warmth. We both slept very nicely. To our dismay, this did not work the next night.

On June 22, we were transferred to a spot directly on the beach that was exposed to a cold wind off the English Channel. Here on the beach, nature called. But where to go, that was the question. I didn't know any English, so I made some up by asking a guard, "Mister, piss?" He answered, "Over there, my boy." And that was my first conversation in English.

That night it was bitter cold. We all lay together like sardines in a can. To help block the wind, we built up a barricade of sand. That helped protect us and we made it through the night without suffering.

Earlier that evening someone told me that if I would like to work, I should stand at the gate early in the morning and something nice would come my way. That I did. Sure enough, a GI was there, calling for ten volunteers. I was the first one; I wanted to be part of this enterprise.

We climbed onto a truck, which took us to the top of a bluff where a field hospital—called a MASH unit—needed to be cleaned of all the trash lying among the tents. Ernie Pyle mentioned this place, too, in his essay, "The Tent City on Top of the Bluff."

Before we went to work, we were treated to a sumptuous breakfast. Well, for us it was; not so much for the GIs. They smelled the soup and dumped it into the already overflowing garbage can. What a waste! We were used to having a rather thin soup for lunch.

After this feast with the soup and other good stuff, everyone was given a bag and told to pick up the litter, mostly paper, around the tents. What else did we find? Lots of packs of cigarettes: open ones minus one or two cigarettes, then discarded. We filled our pockets and soon we had no more room. We could not believe this waste, first with food and now with cigarettes. This could happen only on the winning side.

In the middle of the morning, the Americans served us crackers with a splendid jam, and for lunch, another fine treat. Afterward, we all lay on the ground, full and happy after many days without sufficient nourishment. As we were leaving, they gave us payment of another twenty cigarettes.

That particular day will stick in my mind forever. When we arrived back on the beach early that evening, the other prisoners were in the process of boarding LSTs, large ships for carrying cargo and troops as well as panzers and other vehicles. It was low tide and we sat down on a dirty and rusty floor. Soon afterward we heard the water rising and we sailed away from the continent, away from the war. I curled up in a corner and went to sleep. We were on our way to "Merrie Olde England."

Chapter Nine

Kissing Europe Goodbye

The next morning we were brought up on deck by a large elevator and got our first glimpse of England as we passed the Isle of Wight. All around us were old warships from World War I.

We disembarked in Southampton and were marched through the city, which was heavily patrolled by British soldiers. The British must have been afraid of us because we saw a guard every ten feet. We ended up in a field adjacent to a railroad track and were separated according to our units. The British authorities seemed to know more about our units than we did. We also noticed they had the same kind of discipline that we had in the German Army: very strict.

During our training in Danzig, we were never instructed about what to do or what not to do in captivity. The German soldier was not supposed to be captured; he should fight to his death according to our führer. Shortly after my capture, the German Army "honored" me with an Infantry attack medal, in silver. I never in my twelve days in Normandy attacked anyone. We had retreated every day into the hinterland. But my parents were happy to be notified about the medal because then they knew I was safe.

We waited again for things to happen in our new life, when at last a train pulled up and we were told to board. The cars were not "forty to eight," to which we were accustomed on the other side of the channel, but were nice coaches. So we traveled in bright sunshine quite in style through Greater London until we reached our next destination, a race track called Kempton Park.

All of our tents were in the middle of this race track. The first thing we had to do was strip completely. Our clothes were inspected for hidden objects, and then our belongings were separated into three piles. In the first pile were money, photographs, and anything considered suspicious. We never saw those items again. We were told that the items in the second pile, such as our dog tags and cigarette lighters, would be returned to us when we were discharged from our last POW camp. Our combs and other personal care items, lying in the third pile, were given back to us right away.

I was a little nervous during the procedure because I had in my possession some British money that I had found earlier on one of the captured American soldiers. But no one said a word. Our guards were Germans who had fled before the war; we had the impression they were Jewish. One of them said to a captured soldier, "Did you throw my piano out of the window?"

Wherever we went in Kempton Park, we had to run. We heard it all the time from the young British, *Wollen Sie wohl laufen!*, meaning "You probably want to run!" Nobody enjoyed that very much. Since our only matches had been taken from us, we smokers congregated around this one guard when he lit up his cigarette. After a short time, we all had ours lit, too. The food was rotten, but we were told that the British had a severe food shortage.

All of us were told to fill out a "Card of Capture for Prisoners of War" to let our folks in Germany know that we were in good shape. This notification took nearly two months to arrive; until then, I was listed as "missing in action." My father had been trying to get information about me from the German military authorities. They finally told him I may have been captured.

On June 26 we left Kempton Park with no regrets. We boarded a train and traveled north through town, where we saw lots of damage done by the Luftwaffe, the German air force. The British people discovered our transport and threw stones at the train and made gestures like cutting our throats. We couldn't complain; it was understandable. Hitler had bombed many of their cities, starting with Coventry in the summer of 1940. The bombing escalated that fall into an all-out Blitz throughout England.

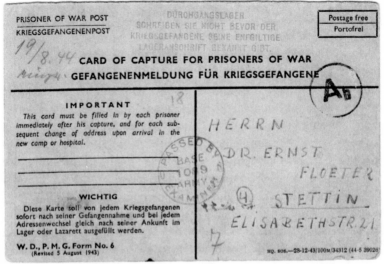

A week after I was captured by the Americans on June 18, 1944, I was asked to fill out the reverse side of this card to let my parents know that I was being held as a prisoner of war.

At last we arrived in the town of Bury, near Manchester. We marched under heavy guard, ten men abreast, to a large factory. We learned we were back in the hands of the Americans. What a relief! For me, it was like a homecoming. I thanked God that I had been captured by an American unit. After my experience at Kempton Park, I didn't have much sympathy for the British.

The factory had a long hall full of bunk beds, and now I made sure I always got an upper berth. There was not much space between the upper and lower bunks, and I couldn't stand any longer to have another guy hanging over me. It had always seemed to work out that way.

We were all pretty hungry, but our American chef in the kitchen told us we wouldn't get as much to eat as we would like until we arrived in the United States. There, we would get plenty to eat. He said here in England the food had to be shipped in by convoy, and nothing could be taken away from the British. "They probably have less than what you have in Germany," he said.

Everything was scarce in our new home, even toilet paper. For that business, we were given two sheets and not more. Well, that wasn't enough, and since the toilets were outside the fence, we had to wait to be called out there once or twice a day.

The day before our departure to America, we were told to shave unless we wanted to stay behind. I think all of us were eager to go. Somehow we could get rid of our stubble in time to qualify for the "cruise" into the blue yonder.

On July 1, we arrived by train in Liverpool, right at the dock, ready to board the big ship SS *Argentina*. It had been built in 1929 in Newport News, Virginia, for the Panama Pacific Line under its original name, SS *Pennsylvania*. Just before we embarked, I slipped, fell to the ground, and thought to kiss the European soil goodbye. We set sail the same day—next stop, America!

We must have been about 3,000 POWs altogether, occupying the lower decks. I had my place in the lowest one, called "E" deck. It was tight above the keel; at least it felt like it. The bunk beds were four-in-one sets. Again, I got an upper one. I had my first taste of the ocean when I mistook a faucet for sweet water and swallowed that brine.

The air in the lower decks was pretty good because smoking was allowed only in the restrooms. Whenever we left our bunks, we had to wear heavy lifesaving jackets. It got very hot, especially when we drank hot coffee at breakfast, lunch, and dinner.

Whatever we got to eat should have been enough, but it wasn't enough for me and not for a lot of other guys, either. I tried to figure out how to get more food. Then I learned the galley always needed dishwashers after dinner, so I became one—but not before I filled up on leftovers. But I didn't last very long standing over the large hot sink, with the water going back and forth, back and forth. I took my leave very fast and went back to my bunk. That experience killed my ambition for more food.

The rules we had to abide by were posted all over the ship and were written by someone who did not have much knowledge of the German language. Signs read: *Wenn Posten sagen HALT, haben Gefangenenzuhalten* and *Alle muessen gehen zu einer physikalischen Untersuchung*. Translated into English, the signs would have read, "When the guard says HALT, everybody had to stand and wait" and "Physical checkup."

Our life on board consisted of being allowed on deck every afternoon for forty-five minutes. Because the sea was very rough, many of the men got a queasy stomach. They would run to the railing, not paying attention to the direction of the wind. The wind would do the rest. What a mess they made! As the old saying goes, "He who spits against the wind gets what he deserves."

Often we were visited by returning GIs who wanted to trade chocolate for our medals, insignia on our uniforms, or anything with a swastika on it. They had left the war behind without any souvenirs. Besides eating, talking, and singing, our pastime was playing blackjack with cigarettes. We had enough of them. One time I ended up with a whole pile and didn't have enough pockets to put them in.

We tried to take showers with our regular soap and wondered in our naïveté why in the world our skin was getting covered with tiny black specks. We didn't know we needed a special soap to shower in salt water. After some complaining, we were issued the right kind of soap. We had to be clean going to the States.

Out on the ocean, the protecting destroyers were bobbing in the heavy seas. Our ship was first in line in this convoy. I could count seventy ships, but there must have been more. One day the ship's cannon started to fire. We thought, "Uh-oh, a German submarine has found us!" But later we were told a floating mine had been sighted.

After twelve days on the Atlantic, an engine stopped one night. A fellow prisoner had been allowed to go up on deck for some reason and came back down all excited with the news that we had landed in America, in New York Harbor. The next morning, we climbed the stairs up to the deck and there it was—my dream fulfilled!

Close to our ship, we saw the ocean liner SS *Ile de France*, one of the first luxury liners built after World War I. Now it was being used to transport troops across the Atlantic.

Our new "masters" didn't let us enjoy solid ground for long. We were led to a ferry that carried us to famous Ellis Island, which thousands of immigrants had passed through on their way to a new future. It was a hot day, but we were standing so close together that no one could have fallen down even if he had fainted.

Soon after we arrived on Ellis Island, we had to strip again. All of our clothes went into a cooker in case any unworthy creatures were still hiding in them. In a large room, the doctors were waiting for us, but first they gave us a bar of soap and a towel and told us to take a shower. What a delight after my last shower back in Baumholder.

The showers onboard ship had not accounted for much. From all of the foxhole digging, the dirt had nearly gone under my skin. It took quite an effort to get rid of it. After that long and enjoyable shower, I went to one of the doctors. He sent me right back where I came from because I still had soap on me. I didn't mind one bit.

After this, everyone got his shots. I don't remember how many, but we got them in both arms at the same time. This was more humane than in the German Army, where we got our shots right in the chest.

We were warned when we left our clothes to be washed that any leather on our uniforms would be destroyed. One guy got his pants back without its leather seat! I left my underwear under a bench; they had done their duty.

In the late afternoon, we left the island and boarded another ferry, this one to take us to Hoboken, New Jersey. What a sight it was passing Manhattan. The skyscrapers were all lit up. There were cars, people, life! It was like Utopia, coming from dark Europe. The thought came to me that many hard-core Nazis would have a hard time believing this sight as they had fixed in their minds a destroyed New York.

In Hoboken, we boarded a train. For us it was a luxurious Pullman, but it was really just a coach to take us to our next destination. We sat three men on four seats, with K rations for everyone and ice water in every car. A guard was stationed at each end. When we had to go to the restroom, we made a sign with our hand since only one prisoner at a time was allowed away from his seat.

As we rode through New York, all of the automobiles at the factories and all of the neon advertising lights made a big impression on me. I could not yet fathom that my dream had come true. That would take another two weeks.

Chapter Ten

The Chance of a Lifetime

It was a beautiful night passing along the Hudson River, discovering West Point, which I had known from a stamp. I kept my eyes open until there was nothing more to see. Early the next morning, a big cloud of vapor suddenly appeared and I knew it came from Niagara Falls. A short time later I saw a British flag flying. Now I was lost. In school I had learned all of the cities, rivers, and mountains in the States, but why were we in Canada? I wanted to end up in the U.S., not Canada. Later on, when I got hold of a map, I found out we had crossed into Ontario. The Canadian authorities had our train doors sealed shut while we traveled through their country.

At last we came to Detroit. An interesting building caught my eye. It was the Ford Rotunda in suburban Dearborn, which reminded me of Centennial Hall, a famous structure in the German city of Breslau, now Wroclaw, Poland. The Rotunda had been built by the Ford Motor Company for the 1933 Chicago World's Fair and later was moved to Dearborn and opened as an exhibition center. Sadly, it was destroyed by fire in 1962.

On this train trip through America, I kept a log of all of the cities and rivers we traveled past or crossed, including the mileage. Other guys were playing cards or sleeping all day long. I couldn't understand why they didn't care where they were going. They had the chance of a lifetime to see something new.

On July 13 at 4:30 in the afternoon, the train stopped. We were at Fort Custer in Battle Creek, Michigan. After entering the POW camp, we assembled and got our instructions from the camp leader, a German POW himself, about the do's and don'ts, especially the don'ts: stay ten feet from the fence because in the guard tower there are some trigger-happy Texans who have a sharp eye out for us; never, under heavy penalty, remove the screens from the windows; and be clean and shower daily. Anybody who got lice would be, in his words, a *Dreckschwein*, a "filthy pig." We now would get to live in a clean environment.

We were assigned to our barracks, which were really something with a shower and restroom in each one, very airy, and clean beds, too. What more could we want? Food. The big question was, what do we get to eat here? When the time came to eat, a whistle sounded and we marched into the mess hall. What a surprise! The tables were filled with food we hadn't seen in a very long time. We were urged to hurry up and get ready for seconds.

The next day we shed our uniforms, or what was left of them, and we got all new clothes, two sets, from head to toe. The only thing I kept was my boots. Our new khaki uniforms had a big "PW" on the back of the shirt as well as on the pants.

Now we had to get registered, which took quite a while. The American staff wanted to know a lot about us, especially if we had any relatives living in the States. We were asked to fill out a card to let our folks know that we were all right.

My interviewer asked me about my profession. I told him I was merely a student, but he didn't believe me. He wanted to know if I had taken any Latin in school. I said "yes," and he had me say the first sentence of Caesar's *Commentarii de Bello Gallico*. Every German student who took Latin had to memorize this part before reading the whole book about the Gallic Wars. I recited it to his satisfaction, and he believed me after that.

Then it was off for more injections and, later, mug shots. Everyone had a number; mine was 31 G 72072. Now we were full-fledged prisoners of war. From then on, I could write letters home.

Twice a day we had to assemble for roll call, where we were counted and informed of any news of concern to us. One time there was a big commotion: a German POW had found his brother, a GI stationed at Fort Custer—while I lost my friend, Werner

Mueller. He had a sore throat and reported to sick bay without saying goodbye, after all of the weeks we had spent together and all of the hectic times we had survived. I have never learned what happened to him.

On July 18 we left Fort Custer and headed west through Chicago, where, to our surprise, the train windows got washed. At 6:30 that evening, we arrived at Camp Ellis, near Peoria, Illinois. We were the first new arrivals there since D-Day. We were "greeted" by German POWs from the Afrika Korps, a group of hard-core Nazi soldiers who had served in North Africa under Field Marshal Erwin Rommel. They had been captured the year before and considered themselves the elite of the German Army. Many of them taunted us with catcalls and shouted at us, "You traitors, you Communists!"

This took me quite by surprise. I thought we had gotten away from the Nazis, but I erred. In every camp, these brutes had their commandos and kangaroo courts. They would make POWs with different political beliefs from theirs get out of bed at night and then condemn them to death, either by hanging or clubbing.

At Camp Ellis, these Nazis told us that our names would be given to the Gestapo after the German victory. A few prisoners got so scared they committed suicide. This threat went on for several months. The Americans said, "We are here to protect you from the outside, but what goes on in the inside is your business."

It finally got out of hand. After many fights and fatalities, special rules were put into place. Everyone whose life was in danger could report for protective custody at the gate, and the perpetrators would be executed. As it turned out, fourteen Afrika Korps POWs in several other camps were courtmartialed and found guilty of murder. They were executed in July and August of 1945 and buried at Fort Leavenworth, Kansas.

But not all of the Afrikan POWs were thugs. The others threatened us only when we tried to tell them the war was lost. These soldiers had been captured away from their homeland and didn't know, or didn't want to know, about the destruction of German cities. They didn't want to believe the daily reports in the newspapers, even the German ones. In their eyes, it was all lies. As long as we kept quiet, they left us alone.

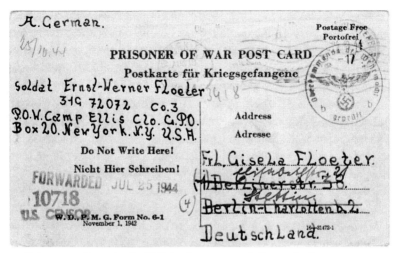

Prisoners of war in the U.S. had to use specially marked stationery to write home. I sent this post card in July, 1944, to my sister, Gisela.

When I went into the PX for the first time, I couldn't believe my eyes. All of the shelves were filled with candy bars, cigarettes, and other goodies. A pack of twenty cigarettes cost twenty cents; a bottle of Coke or Pepsi was a nickel. I had no money, but the "old" inhabitants were millionaires to me because they worked every day as barbers, cooks, shoemakers, and pastry makers and got paid eighty cents a day. They were rich!

I tried to find a good fellow who would spend some money on me, and I found one. He bought me a candy bar, a little pocket English dictionary, and a German-English dictionary that became my most precious possession besides an old almanac.

Although there were rules about our clothing, the POWs who had been there for some time had been allowed to fashion their pants with extra-wide pant legs, and they wore Afrika Korps field caps. To our amazement, POWs even had the right to strike. We could hardly believe this was possible in a prisoner of war camp. I wonder what would have happened to the American and other Allied prisoners in Germany if they had tried this.

Five men from our barracks were always hungry, including me. There simply was not enough food in our kitchen. It didn't help that the cooks and their help did not economize in any way. Even here, the

51

waste of war was very visible. We found out that if we went over after lunch or dinner to a kitchen that served the Afrikans and offered our help, we would get lots of leftovers. The cooks predicted that after two weeks we would have enough to eat with just the first helping in our own mess hall, and they were so right.

The camp itself was kept in excellent shape, with many flowers and sculptures. We had in our ranks many artistically inclined men. One had made it his hobby to catch hummingbirds, which were quite numerous, and mount them in glass caches. I would rather have seen them alive. He did the same thing with big, beautiful moths.

We had work to do, too, if one could call it work. One day we had to clean a clubhouse, and the next day we were driven to a big overgrown lawn. Everyone who was given an American scythe made an effort to do the job, but the implement was so different from German scythes that even the German farmers had trouble handling them.

Then we were issued sickles with a honing stone. I had never used a sickle before in my life. These worked out better, but I think we spent more time sharpening than cutting. The guards didn't care as long as we behaved in an orderly manner. So far, our life in America was very good. Our treatment as well as the food were better than anyone ever would have thought.

Chapter Eleven

"Have You Had Your Candy Already?"

We left Camp Ellis on July 29 by truck and ended up in Eureka, Illinois, a college town with tree-lined streets and a good-sized park in front of the Eureka College gymnasium. It was the same college President Ronald Reagan had attended in 1928-1932.

The gym became our home for the next six weeks. It was filled with bunk beds, with our duffle bags stored out on a balcony. The kitchen and mess tent were located behind the building. We were located right in the middle of town, with only two guards and a single wire fence surrounding our "camp."

It was here I became friends with Thomas Kramer, one of the cooks. By trade, he was a cigar maker. We would spend the rest of our POW stay together.

Every night we all sat outside, singing old German songs. It didn't take much time for the street in front of us to begin filling up with German-Americans who came from far away to hear us. This part of the country had been settled primarily by Germans. The city put up "no parking" and "no loitering" signs, but they came in droves nevertheless.

The food for everyone was prepared in the kitchen, even for the guards. Their meals were cooked the American way, but they said they preferred the German food. We could also buy beer (!), but we were told in no uncertain terms that we were not allowed to take it outside; *never*, because Eureka was a dry town. That was something new to us, too.

One fellow prisoner wanted to lead a choir and asked for volunteers. Lacking anything else to do, I joined and had great fun. Our commanding officer told us we could go back to work once we had sung "Brahms's Lullaby," but not before. So we practiced until August 8, my birthday, and that evening we sang it. The kitchen always baked a special cake for the birthday fellow; I had to get my buddies to help me finish it off.

Later that night we started to work at a corn cannery called Libby, McNeill & Libby. It was located in the nearby town of Washington. Each night about 9:30, a big truck came to camp and transported us to the cannery. The corn the farmers had picked during the day was delivered here. We had to operate a machine that cut off the end of the ears as well as the husks. It was a rather monotonous job, but really not bad at all. During our breaks—every twenty minutes—we had a chance to talk with the civilian workers. As in Eureka, many of them were of German origin.

Depending on the weather, we worked mostly until one or two in the morning. The management was very happy with our performance on the job. Once in a while we worked so fast that the whole operation came to a standstill.

We wondered what the end product of our work could be, so one night we went over to one of the big cooling vats filled with cans, took a can back with us, and opened it up. We found out what it was—creamed corn. We had known this before only as chicken feed. Eating it, we found we liked it very much.

On Sundays a German-American pastor came to worship with us. The first time he visited, he was hard to understand because he had not spoken German in thirty years. But he improved after coming back two more times.

Finally it was payday. We earned eighty cents for each working day and ten cents for the days we didn't work. Now I could live! I bought some tobacco, Velvet. To this day, whenever I smell Velvet, it brings me right back. It's funny how a particular smell can take you back to a special time.

One time during roll call, our lieutenant needed a number of

POWs to transfer to another camp. I said to myself, "No, that's not for me. I like it here too much." As it turned out, it was good that I stayed in Eureka because of what was to come.

When the corn picking was done, the cannery closed for the season and our time in Eureka came to an end. Those six weeks were like a vacation. The weather was perfect; the food, excellent; and the treatment, terrific. I knew I wouldn't mind living there one day. But on September 6, we packed up our few belongings, boarded the trucks, and off we went on another adventure.

We traveled northward to Rockford, Illinois, to Camp Grant. At least 3,000 German POWs occupied this camp. It was divided into several parts by single fences one could crawl through. Here I found the only person from my hometown who was also a POW in America. On top of that, he had been a patient of my father's a few years earlier. We talked for a while, but he was older than I and we went our separate ways.

Now we had to live in tents, six men to a tent. I had a new friend, Lohse, from Munich-Gladbach. He was a likable fellow who wanted to solve the problem of the perpetuum mobile, which is motion that, once started, continues on its own. This was on his mind all of the time. I hope he gave it up later on.

Camp Grant was a good place to be. We had a library, pool hall, bands, and a theater with male actors. The performances were very funny. Besides that, we had fun with other tent members by hiding their beds and engaging in water battles. Several days went by before we were told the type of work we would be doing.

For the job I was assigned, I had to get up very early, nearly dawn. I'm not an early riser, but sometimes, as in this case, one has no other choice—at least, that was what I thought as a law-abiding prisoner.

Soon I was accustomed to the sunrise job. It meant riding in a truck for quite a while, passing through Belvedere and Cherry Valley, to a large potato field. Then off to potato picking, but not by hand, which was what everybody thought it would be. Instead, we saw a tractor, driven by a Japanese man, pulling a motorized picker.

Standing on the platform of the picker were five men sorting out the sand and dirt from the spuds and placing them on a conveyor belt. This would be my job. I did this with just one hand at first and was told, "Use two hands!"

Then the potatoes were bagged. I did that once; it was a bad job. I couldn't keep up with the speed of the conveyor. The potatoes came too fast, and continuously lifting the heavy bags was not for me.

One time someone put sugar in the gas tank of the tractor, and we had to wait a couple of hours until it was repaired. Doing this was not right since we were being treated humanely, but some other fellows felt differently.

We found out there was a cucumber field not too far away. We asked the guard if we could go there as long as he came along. "No," he said, "you go alone." He knew no one would run away. We enjoyed the fresh vegetables.

Every day during our lunch break, a Cadillac drove up. Out of it came a prosperous older couple. Since we were picking the potatoes for the Curtiss Candy Company, I assumed the gentleman, of German origin, was the owner. (The Curtiss Candy Company was founded in 1916 by Otto Schnering of Chicago. Schnering used his mother's maiden name for the company as German-sounding names were not popular in America during World War I.) His wife, a very nice lady with lots of makeup, would give every one of us a Baby Ruth candy bar, saying each time, "Have you had your candy already?"

This was a new treat for me. There were no candy bars like Baby Ruth or Three Musketeers in Germany. The candy bars there were all milk chocolate or dark chocolate.

One morning I did not feel like getting up, so I didn't report for work. No one cared. That afternoon Lohse and I caught a truck on its way to a corn cannery near New Rochelle. We didn't do anything there except run around and wait for the return trip.

The only thing that made me angry at Camp Grant was hearing some of the other POWs call our Jewish-American commander "a dirty Jew." Despite all of the terrible things Germany had done and was doing to the Jewish people, he treated us very well. If he got any requests for musical instruments or props for the theater, he agreed right away. He didn't have to be nice to us, but he was, like most Americans, a very generous human being.

Ernst W. Floeter

One day a rumor went around that all of us would be leaving soon. We asked the guards if they knew anything, but they only said something about cotton picking, whatever that was. It was early October and the weather had turned very cold. We donned the winter clothes we had been given back at Camp Ellis—drab green U.S. Army uniforms without the insignia—and waited for the next episode.

Chapter Twelve

The Art of Picking Cotton

I was spared a cold winter in the northern states as the train we boarded at 4:30 p.m. on October 10 headed south. My guardian angel was with me again because when it comes to working outside in the cold, I am an icicle. Again, we were very comfortable with three men on four seats. It was a beautiful train, and the whistle had a majestic sound; it affected me emotionally.

I had a window seat and watched where we were going throughout the entire trip. I made notes of all of the cities and rivers. We passed through St. Louis, Missouri, and Little Rock, Arkansas, into Texas. Then, in the middle of nowhere, the train stopped and we could all get off to stretch our legs. A snake—for many, the first one they had ever seen—was disturbed by us and fled. Perhaps it knew we were the enemy!

It became warmer and warmer outside, but the heat on the train kept right on going. During the night at a switchyard, our train was banged around onto another track. The railway workers were not very careful of the passengers.

Passing by San Antonio, I was really taken in by the palm trees and Mexican-style houses. I thought, "I would like to live here." Then, going through oil country, we passed by what looked like a forest of oil derricks.

By nightfall we approached the Mexican border close to Del

Rio on the Rio Grande River. We were all quite surprised when we crossed the high bridge over the Pecos River gorge. Along the border we passed many border control stations.

I went to sleep when it became too dark for me to see the "new world" around us. As soon as the sun rose and I could see where we were going, a desolate landscape greeted us.

Seeing lots of petrified mud hills, I began to look for a wall that signified the end of the world. Then, by golly, the first cotton fields appeared along the way. The guard at Camp Grant was right! At 7:45 a.m. on October 13, we arrived at Fort Bliss in Texas. Here, we stood in the heat for five hours with our winter clothes on until we started on our next adventure in an open truck. On the way, the guards stopped and refreshed themselves with ice cream. It was nice to see them enjoying it. At 3:45 p.m., we arrived at our destination—Hatch, New Mexico. We were all pretty thirsty. I think I drank three Cokes.

Hatch is an agricultural town, with an elevation of 4,078 feet and about 1,600 souls. Now I was in the middle of the "old West." Nearly every boy in Germany dreamt of this part of the United States. I had read many stories, both fact and fiction, about Indians and cowboys when I was younger, especially those by one German author, Karl May. He wrote quite a few books about this time in history even though, at the time of his writing, he had never set foot in America. My cowboy movie idol was Tom Mix. Now, my dream had come true, but what lay ahead of me was *work*.

As we came into camp, our new ruler, Lieutenant Theodore Strutz, greeted us. Soon we would find out what he was really like. Our second in command was an Italian officer whom we simply called "Itaka." He was a rather likable fellow.

The rectangular-shaped camp consisted of five barracks for sixty men (really boys) each; a recreation hall with a piano; a PX; a kitchen with a mess hall; a first-aid station; a repair shop for the tailor, shoemaker, and blacksmith; and an office. We also had a barbershop, a washroom with showers, and a restroom with about eight stools. Officers Strutz and Itaka lived outside the fence in a brick building; it was where we had to go to pick up our packages so that we could open them in front of them. Alongside that building were the kitchen and the mess hall for the guards. Their barracks sat across the street in front of a school yard. The guards were of various nationalities—Mexican, Indian, and German as well as American.

A number of Germans POWs worked inside the camp. Sergeant Karl Harmann was our German-English interpreter. Jupp Smith, a monk, served as our medic. He had PP, for Protective Personnel, stenciled on his clothing instead of the PW we had on our clothes (except for our socks). There was a German plumber, too, who was busy once in a while when someone plugged up the sewer.

We slept in bunk beds, and two big potbellied stoves heated our barracks in the winter; one fellow had to get up very early to start the fire. Outside was a big pile of coal. At least we had enough of that and didn't have to freeze.

Beside my bed, which was comfortable, I set up an orange crate as a nightstand. I used an old flour bag as a curtain, then put my belongings inside it, like books and photographs. I placed my clothes in a duffel bag the Americans had given each of us. It had my name and number on it and hung from the end of my bed. I slept with my head away from the light, so I fastened a mirror behind me to reflect light from the lamp onto whatever book I was reading.

My best friends—Thomas Kramer, Otto Gollnow, Joseph Goebbels, Gerhard Brokuff, and Adolf Abel—had their bunks near my "living quarters." We were all anti-Nazis and hoped for a defeat of the Nazis in Germany. We would go to the PX to buy Coca Cola, Pepsi Cola, candy, cigarettes, beer, soap, and other toiletries. I liked Pepsi better than Coke because the bottle was twice the size for the same price. In the winter we could buy ice cream for twenty cents a pint. We couldn't get it in the summer because there was no refrigeration to keep it frozen.

We had to wash our own clothing, which I usually did on Saturday nights. We were supplied with laundry soap, but if we ran out of that, we used Palmolive or some other good soap. In the middle of camp, right behind the gate, was the place for our twice-daily roll calls. If roll call was taken in the middle of a haircut, you had to get out of the chair and show up.

Surrounding our camp was a tall barbed wire fence with one guard tower on the east side. One day we had to strengthen the west side of the fence with more barbed wire. While visiting Camp Hatch years later in 1977, I found a large coil of barbed wire hanging there. I took a picture of it. I assume it was the same roll.

Many gardens occupied the area south of the fence. A goat lived there and if it stood on top of a little hill, we would say, *Die Hip steht auf dem Berg*, which meant "The goat is on the hill," or that rain is coming.

A bit farther south stood one of the many churches in town. This was another surprise to us—finding so many different denominations. We were used to having only two in Germany, Evangelical Lutheran and Catholic. Every two weeks at Hatch, a Lutheran pastor from El Paso came to give us some support. He read to us a little and was very kind. A Catholic priest visited us every couple of weeks, too.

We never saw German officers who were held as POWs; they were kept apart from us. Under the rules of the Third Geneva Convention, captured officers didn't have to work. Even so, they were paid more than our eighty cents a day.

Our cotton picking job started on October 16. My first farmer was Mr. Maguire (or McGuire) in Salem. Every morning he greeted me with "Hello, Floeter." He introduced us to the "art" of picking cotton. The important thing, he said, was to pick the cotton clean. The bushes were four to five feet high, and when the buds were open, they looked like snowed-over Christmas trees. The fields were a beautiful sight.

For two weeks the work was hard on our backs. After we got used to it, Strutz imposed a quota system. In the first harvest, each of us had to pick 220 pounds of cotton, which amounted to two big bags and part of a third. We were able to get it done if the farmer's cotton was low to the ground and full. But if we arrived at a new field and saw the goal was not possible, we urged the farmer to go to him and tell him that we'll pick as much as we can and do a good job. This meant plucking every fiber out of the bolls.

Most of the time, the farmer came back with good news, but sometimes not. So, we did what we had to do to increase the weight in order to achieve the quota. Today, I would say I am sorry that we had to do this and cheat the farmer. But we had to look out for ourselves. When we returned to camp, Strutz always knew how much we had picked, and he would punish us if we hadn't met the quota.

With Strutz as the boss, we all became pretty edgy, never knowing what he had in mind. Food became more scarce, and every evening at roll call he gave long "sermons" that we had to endure. One night he told us that his ancestors were officers in the Prussian Army, which made him pretty proud. But the next night he would say he condemned the hour when his mother brought him into this world as a German. We never knew if he could understand or speak the German language as he always had a translator.

Because of his red hair, somebody came up with the nickname of "Red Dog." One night at roll call, the searchlights went dark. Nobody moved. After a while, they came back on and Red Dog announced that he had given the guards orders to shoot if we had moved.

The farmers liked him because they could make deals with him. If a farmer needed help, he was supposed to put in his order days before he needed it. But if a farmer brought fruit or some other gift to Strutz, the farmer could get help the same day.

Our workday started about 8 a.m. After roll call, the different pickup trucks came and took us out to the fields. Very rarely would the guard bother to look after us. Mostly, he sat down in the shade and told us to tell him if the lieutenant showed up. We would pick the cotton, dragging a six-foot-long bag between our legs, until noon. For our thirty-minute lunch break, we had sandwiches, some fruit, and water.

As long as the sun was shining, it was warm. But in the winter, when the sun disappeared behind the mountains at four p.m., it got cold and my hands would start to freeze. That was one good thing in my life—I was sent to the Southwest, where it was mostly warm and even hot, and not to an area in the North.

When we came back to camp each day, we had to pass by Strutz as he was examining the worksheet where the farmer (or a guard) had penciled in next to our names the number of pounds we had picked. If we hadn't picked enough, he would ask, "Why didn't you pick more?" One time, someone said, "Rheumatism, Sir." The next POW came up with the same excuse. When Strutz got to the third name, he said, "You have rheumatism, too?"

One evening, while the whole camp was out picking cotton for Mr. Francois, known as the "Cotton King," something happened to cause Lieutenant Strutz to come out to the field. He made us march back to camp. He ordered silence, but someone started to sing, and as punishment he shut down the PX for several days.

A strike was called for Monday. On that morning, we all stayed in bed instead of going outside to an assembly. It didn't take too long before the guards came into the barracks and chased us out into a high school sports field across from camp. Here we sat all day Monday while the officers, including some from Fort Bliss, talked about what to do with us. We were all nervous because we didn't know what was going to happen.

By late afternoon, we were hungry and thirsty. That evening we were told that if we went back to our barracks and reported for work Tuesday morning, the PX would be opened. We were happy. Lieutenant Strutz told our German leader that he should have chased us into the desert and let us stay out there over night, where we would not have survived the cold. It bothered him that he had given in, so his treatment from then on became harsher.

About twelve in our group were "super Nazis," those who still believed Germany would win the war. They denounced everything that was written in the newspapers, which we received almost daily. My buddies and I tried to stay away from them. One good thing our lieutenant did was to send them into the desert each morning and make them dig holes. We liked that. One day in the recreation room one of them played the Hitler Youth Anthem on the piano. The next day a truck carried the instrument out to the desert, and he had to play this song over and over all day long. We were happy that something had happened to one of that group.

Chapter Thirteen

Censorship on Both Sides

One of my best memories of Camp Hatch was the music. The intercom played a lot of good American songs like "Chattanooga Choo Choo" and "Lullaby of Broadway." Also, one of the fellows in our group, Anton Schappe, was quite a classical pianist. He got hold of some sheet music and whenever he played, I always sat beside him. I especially remember him playing "The Bells of St. Mary's."

I never learned to read music myself, but I grew up with classical music and German marches. My folks had about thirty 78 rpm records that we played on our wind-up gramophone. We also had season tickets to the symphony orchestra in Stettin, which I enjoyed very much; it sounded so majestic. There was always good music on the radio, too.

Movies were an exciting and well-greeted diversion in our camp life. Generally, we had one every week. We all got ready for the event when the news came, "The movie is here!" We usually sat inside, but sometimes outside. Quite often we couldn't understand the plot, but who cared? Once in while, a German explanation came with it or, if it was a war movie, one could follow the story. It so happened that one week the camp leaders forgot to get us a movie, so the next week we had two, which kept us up until midnight. The movies did cost us—ten whole cents.

We saw thirty-four movies in all. Some of my favorites were *Back to Bataan, Abe Lincoln Goes to Washington, Edison*, the Bob Hope "road" movies, and movies about the war in the Pacific. These were much more realistic than the newsreels we had seen in Germany.

But no popcorn. We didn't know what popcorn was. We brought corn in from the fields at corn-picking time, and it became our main staple later on when food got scarcer and scarcer. Every night we would roast corn, eat, and talk—mostly about women and how we would punish Hitler, awful things that we would do to him. We ate corn in the morning, too. Out in the fields, we roasted the ears over a fire and feasted on them during the day. They tasted *so* good.

When Thanksgiving came that year, it was a holiday for us, too. We had no idea what it was all about, but we were glad to have the day off. A Methodist church behind our camp had a picnic with a big table full of food, giving us our first impression of this American tradition. We had our own turkey, too, in the mess hall.

On December 14, our squad was working for several days at a cotton field close to camp. We played around too much, not knowing our guard would report us to the lieutenant. So that day Strutz came out at 10 a.m. We had to weigh our bags, which were pretty empty. Only one of us had more than the others.

We had to march back to camp and then to the police station in town to get a calaboose. This was an iron cage, seven by seven by seven, which we had to drag to a spot just outside camp. It became our home for three nights. We were lucky, though. We had our winter coats and were given water and bread. During the day we were allowed to sit outside in front of it. We were supplied a pail for our business, but nobody used it and that made the lieutenant furious. When he saw the empty pail, he grabbed a rifle from the guard and fired a shot, just missing our squad leader.

The first night there were twelve of us; the next night, fourteen; and the last night, sixteen. It became quite crowded. The next morning was a Sunday and we were released. We were pretty hungry and for breakfast we got pancakes. After that, we showered and went to sleep. From then on, every evening when the Italian officer had roll call, he asked, "How many men in the calaboose?" When the answer was "None," he said, "Fine."

Just before Christmas, the lieutenant asked us if we would like to have a Christmas tree. A rousing "Yes" was the answer. He asked us if we wanted to have turkey. Another rousing "Yes." Then he asked if we were going to pick 220 pounds of cotton. A rousing "No" was the answer this time. He knew he would get us for that.

About this time three or four guys walked off and left camp. It was a rather stupid thing to do. The New Mexico State Police began looking for them on their motorcycles. After four days, the POWs gave up and were put in the calaboose without their coats. Our lieutenant gave them two weeks with only water and bread. When they came out, they looked like people from Auschwitz.

For Christmas, we got a nice tall tree from Silver City, New Mexico, and turkey for our holiday meal. In our barracks, we sang the German Christmas carol *O du frohliche* ("O How Joyfully") and *Stille Nacht* ("Silent Night"). The Red Cross gave us shaving cream and German cigarettes. The Red Cross meant well, but there was not much taste to the cigarettes compared to American ones. We thought about home and hoped that everyone was alive and all right. We had had no news in six months—not since before the Normandy invasion.

In Germany, our tradition was to celebrate Christmas over two days—Christmas Day at home with family and the next day visiting grandparents—but Christmas was celebrated on only one day in America. I hoped for rain so we wouldn't have to go work on December 26. Then a miracle happened . . . suddenly I heard raindrops falling on the roof. It rained hard and soon the fields were under water. This meant no work until the next calendar year.

The new year, 1945, came with the hope that we would be home by the next Christmas. From reading the newspapers, we knew how the war was going. The Russians were coming closer to Berlin in the east, and the Allies were closing in on the western front.

In January, the first mail arrived. It had taken three months for it to come from Germany. I received my mail on the sixteenth. I got so much from my parents and family and friends that I felt a little embarrassed. Some fellows did not get much mail. In all, I got thirty-two letters.

We could even get packages, but these had to be opened in front of an officer to see if they contained canned food. If a POW did receive food, he could pick it up just one can at a time from the kitchen. I received a few books, which I later gave to the library.

We could write one letter and one post card each week. These, too, took three months to reach Germany. We had to be careful of what we wrote because the mail was censored on both sides. One side cut out what wasn't allowed, and the other side blacked it out. Sometimes a letter would consist of one big hole.

Taken at Camp Hatch, New Mexico, in 1945, this is the only picture of me as a prisoner of war. I am nineteen years old. We wore U.S. Army-issue khaki shirts, but without the insignia.

The cotton harvest ended in February with the picking of the unopened cotton bolls. I had picked 5,503 pounds of cotton over seventy-five days that season and earned $59.57. When frost hits the cotton fields, the cows come in to graze. We would joke that after feeding on what was left in the fields, the cows would expel cotton stockings! During this time we would occasionally have snow, just enough for a snowball fight. By 10 a.m. it would vanish.

We had this one fellow in our midst named Gerd Findeisen. To this day I wonder if he was a *bona fide* prisoner or just pretending to be. He wore the same uniform as we did, but he spoke fluent American English, did no work at all, and went in and out of camp at will. He said he came from a wealthy German family. One day he came around and asked me if I was a Nazi. I gave him a clear answer: "For heaven's sake, NO!" He wrote down my name and went on his way.

A bit later my buddies and I got together with him. He promised us heaven on earth—that all fifteen of us would be pulled out of camp and sent to work at an airport as almost free men. This kept our hopes up for the next month as he assured us several more times. But nothing ever came of it.

Then spring came to Hatch. Lieutenant Strutz started looking for work for us. There were several large trees around camp and he didn't like them. So he supplied us with steel wedges and a two-man saw. Both of these were new to me, especially the saw. All went well until one fellow got hit in the eye by a steel splinter from one of the wedges. That did it—no more cutting down trees.

Then we were supposed to do cleanup around the camp. Well, we did it all right. Whenever the lieutenant showed his face, we grabbed a broom and tried to look busy. One day we had to clean the back of the bar. We smiled after finding some bottles with a little liquor inside of them.

The most unpleasant work we had to do was cleaning the levees on the Rio Grande River. These were sand embankments overgrown with weeds; nothing had been done with them in ages. Here the guards were members of the Corps of Engineers—and regular tyrants. It was hard work, and if we stopped to catch our breath, the guards were on us immediately. Thank heavens, this work lasted only two days.

One of our "benefactors" was the bank president, Mr. Johnston. We had to build a small house for him out of cinder blocks, and he always put out a large can of tobacco for our use. Back at camp, the good brand of cigarettes we liked sometimes were in short supply, and then we got Pall Malls. Nobody liked them. When it got really tough, we bought tobacco leaves in a pouch. Oh, they were bad! In order to smoke the stuff, I had to wash the leaves and remove the juice. One could make cigars from them, and some guys smoked them in their pipes early in the morning. That was not for me.

Even though we had enough coal at camp to last a long time, one day we went to the rail yard where there was a whole freight car filled with coal. All of it had to be brought back to camp by truck. That was a job. But it got done, and when evening came, we were all clean again. We heard that the townspeople complained that we used too much water. But with the southwestern heat, we had to shower at least once and sometimes twice a day.

One day our lieutenant got the idea that we could build a football field out in the desert near the train station. That sounded interesting and I went to work on the morning shift. On our first day, a guard showed us the secret of how to survive in the desert. He chopped open a barrel cactus that had cool water inside and we tasted it. It was not the best of water, but it didn't matter if one was very thirsty. Of course, a heavy instrument was needed to cut open the cactus.

At noon we rode back to camp, taking our tools with us. When the afternoon shift arrived in the desert and the lieutenant learned the tools were not there (he probably knew this all along), these guys had to march all afternoon, without a break, from one bridge to another over the Rio Grande. He rode in a truck in front of the group, his machine gun in his hand, watching over the tired marchers.

This was just another dirty trick Lieutenant Strutz played on us. We didn't trust him, but at least we knew that we were going to get home. I don't believe we ever finished that football field project.

Chapter Fourteen

"Thank Heavens, It's Over!"

On the evening of April 12, 1945, we learned at roll call that President Franklin D. Roosevelt had passed away. One of the Nazi POWs, who was standing beside me, said, "Now we win the war! The swine is dead!" I thought, "Oh, what an idiot!"

The same thing happened when we learned that Hitler was dead. This POW blurted out that Germany would still win the war. These misguided men were so brainwashed and indoctrinated in Nazi ideology that they couldn't comprehend what was really happening. On May 8, when we learned the war in Europe had ended, all of these fellows disappeared into a corner, withdrawing in defeat.

That same day, V-E Day, May 8, I broke my glasses playing soccer, and Itaka took me to Fort Bliss to get new ones. As we drove in a Jeep through Las Cruces, we were greeted with the famous victory sign from people who were happily viewing a triumphal parade. We were happy, too, and responded with the same victory sign. Thank heavens, we all thought, it's over!

At Fort Bliss, I sat in the optometrist's waiting room among a bunch of GIs. I almost felt like one of them. It was quite an adventure for me to be there among all of the hustle and bustle of camp life at Fort Bliss compared to the relatively quiet atmosphere in Hatch. Soon I got my new glasses and vowed not to engage in any more soccer games.

Later that month, the field work began again. The cotton was growing—and the weeds, too. For the next four months our job was to hoe the weeds to help many of the nearby farmers. This work was not too bad.

My first farmer that spring was Mr. Mundy, who showed me how to hoe. After watching me for a while, he said, "Pretty good." It sounded more like "Purry good," and I, with my meager English, wasn't sure what he had said until sometime later. We had a good time on Mr. Mundy's farm as the guard left us in peace.

In the middle of the farmland under a copse of trees—which we called the "bush"—we ate our lunch in the shade. It would get very hot and the irrigation ditches suited us very much. We waded right into them with all of our clothes on to cool off. Sometimes we would ask the guard if he would allow us to swim in one of the large ditches or even in the river. But his typical answer was, "Not today; maybe tomorrow."

Well, we did it anyway when he was far away. We stripped down, first making sure nobody was around who could see what the German POWs were doing, and enjoyed a swim. I recall the nice atmosphere in June when the red-winged blackbirds were singing. There must have been a lot of snakes around because sometimes a farmer, in a playful mood, would throw a nonpoisonous snake at us to scare us. We encountered only one rattler while we were out in the fields. I never saw it, but I heard that one of my comrades had dispatched it.

Besides the hard work of picking cotton, our life was not so bad. But one day, shortly after May 8, a large part of our food supply was picked up and taken away. This happened in all of the POW camps, but our dear lieutenant cut our rations even further.

We had been taking a salt tablet every morning, but Strutz stopped this. He also cut back on the salt in our food and eventually eliminated it altogether. Everything we ate tasted like we had boiled our socks. It was just another thing the lieutenant did to punish us. Once in a while the farmers took pity on us and, as we were leaving for the day, threw a bag of salt to us so the guard would not see it.

One farm couple, Mr. and Mrs. Hitchcock in Salem, had a field that seemed to be at the end of civilization. To the north of the farm was an embankment where no man's land began. I had the wish to go up there and see what lay behind, but I didn't dare as it might have looked as though I was trying to escape.

We picked their chili peppers and in one shed found a big pile of chili powder. I took some and put it on my food. It helped. With all of the sweating we did each day, the lack of salt didn't do us any good. Mrs. Hitchcock tried to refresh us every noon with a bowl of Jello.

All of the farmers were supposed to bring us enough water, and most of them were very faithful about it. But one day, when it was very hot and sand was blasting through the air, we had no water. I couldn't stand it. The river was close by, so I walked over to it and put my face into the water and drank some. At that point, I didn't care what might be in the water. But nothing happened; no aftereffects. I wouldn't do this today.

One of the nicer jobs we had was picking tomatoes. They were so beautiful! I was always on the lookout for vitamin C in any form, so I ate them from morning until noon. About that time each day I figured I had better stop because my skin would begin to shrivel.

One morning during that summer, July 16, we were awakened at 5:30 by the sound of a tremendous explosion. We had heard so many bombs during the war that we didn't think much of it. If we had gone outside, we would have seen the huge mushroom cloud. It was the world's first test of an atomic bomb—just sixty miles from our camp. The first news reports to the public said the noise was caused by an ammunitions magazine that had blown up. Later we would learn that it was the beginning of the Atomic Age.

The cotton was growing, the blooms were turning to bolls, and another harvest was ready. On September 19, I tied a sack around my belly and went off into the "fun." Even though we were experienced pickers, the sharp corners on the cotton still stung. We soothed the pain with glycerine.

One day, shortly after our return to camp, we were all called outside. "What is happening now?" we wondered. The farmer we had worked for had just returned from the cotton gin, and his wagon was filled with all kinds of stuff—stones, tire rims, etc.—that we had used to increase the weight of the cotton. We were lucky; our wages were cut only for that day. I hope the farmer was given the difference.

The corn was also ready for harvest, and we roasted corn each night in camp. Still, hunger was our number one problem. Every evening three buddies and I went to the fence across from the American kitchen and hoped that Walter, the cook for the officers and guards, would bring out some leftovers for us four hungry souls. We felt like beggars, but we really didn't care.

One night the lieutenant told me to bring him "water." In my eagerness, I came back with a pail of water. No, he said, he wanted Walter, the cook. So much for my English.

If a farmer was happy with our work, he would reward us afterwards with a chocolate bar or some other treat. On my birthday, August 8, I worked for Mr. Algarez, and he presented each of us with a huge watermelon at the end of the day. We ate and ate, filling our bellies.

That fall took a rather peaceful course except for one incident. Strutz, in one of his bizarre moods, decided to turn off the electricity for several nights. So in order to have some light, we went to the PX and bought anything that would burn with a wick, like hair tonic and aftershave lotion. Sure, it smelled terrible, but it was great fun, too.

Soon afterwards, a sign from heaven was in the air. Our blacksmith, Hermann Riesebeck, from Greifswald, got an order from Lieutenant Strutz to build him a trailer and lamp out of an old wrought iron bed. Was Red Dog going away? One night we came back to camp and got the good news: Strutz was gone! There was great jubilation.

Two new officers came to replace Strutz, but they didn't last long—probably because they were too good to us. Now we were in store for the next one: Lieutenant Dolozic. He was a soldier through and through. When he came to roll call, he marched from his house as though he were on a parade ground.

Dolozic was the opposite of Strutz—no more deals with the farmers. One farmer told us that the old lieutenant was good for them but bad for us, and the new one is good for us but bad for them. No more nightly sermons either; it was strictly business with Lieutenant Dolozic. One time he slapped a prisoner in the face for putting Nazi insignias on his shirt.

During the fall he had us fill out the same questionnaire every two weeks. It contained all kinds of questions concerning our past in Germany. He compared our answers to see if they were consistent, so we had to remember what we wrote the last time. But Lieutenant Dolozic knew we were the good guys.

The last mail from my sister came in late fall. She wrote that everyone at home was all right, but that my parents were now living in a little fishing village near the Baltic Sea called Lubmin, in the Soviet Zone, where my father was practicing dentistry. They had fled from the Russians in March of 1945, leaving behind nearly everything they owned.

Our father was lucky he had not been forced into the German Army because later in the war anyone who could walk was a prospective soldier, young or old. He had a lung ailment that kept him from serving.

Christmas came and went. We hoped to be home by the next Christmas, 1946, which we felt was likely to happen. To keep up our morale, we tried to make some alcoholic beverages. We put orange juice and sugar in some bottles and stashed them under the floorboards next to my bed. But on New Year's Eve a rumor went around that the lieutenant had learned our secret. We had to drink the concoction fast. It was too soon for fermentation to have taken place, and the beverage was anything but alcoholic.

Chapter Fifteen

Like Free People

The year 1946 had begun. I added up that I had picked 19,863 pounds and earned a total of $275.63. I already had $72.33 in a trust fund. (In 1947, I was paid in reichsmarks, just before the new money, the deutschmark, came out. It was too bad we weren't paid in deutschmarks; one could not buy much with the old currency.)

In the afternoon of January 9, two trucks with more German POWs came into our camp. What is this all about? There is no room for more. After a short time, the names of those who were to be ready for transport in two hours were read over the intercom. As soon as the first name was read, I knew it was our group. "What a relief," I thought. "Hopefully, something good will happen."

Even though I had been treated well by the people in Hatch, liked the climate very much, and, most importantly, had survived, I was glad to be going on another adventure. During my fifteen months in Hatch and my time in Illinois before that, I had developed a heartfelt liking for this country, which I hoped to see again.

The night of our departure was cold. We picked up one additional German POW in Las Cruces and ended up in Ysleta, Texas. It was dark when we arrived at our new camp. The next morning as I stepped outside the barracks, I beheld a magnificent sight. Everything was covered with hoarfrost, and the air was so clear, one could see far into Mexico.

That first day, I learned the kitchen was looking for some help.

I volunteered—with the result that I was on "kitchen patrol" for the duration of our stay. The bad thing was that I had to get up very early. The good thing was that I had enough to eat. And, it was better to have something to do than nothing at all.

Although I had come a long way since my awkward months as a soldier in France, I had not completely polished my image: I met a fellow POW at Ysleta who was a Catholic priest and asked him how his wife was. I was dumb!

I believe it was at Camp Ysleta that the Lutheran pastor from El Paso, who had come to Hatch every other Sunday, gave his last service before he passed away. We had such a good time with him. He always wished he could take us to his home to sing old German songs, but this remained a dream.

I worked at Ysleta until our last day, the second of March. At 8:30 in the morning, we walked to the railway station. Our train trip began at 9:20 a.m., taking us northeast through Texas, Arkansas, Kentucky, Ohio, and West Virginia to Fort Eustis in Newport News, Virginia. It was a beautiful ride. We were very comfortable and could sleep anywhere we wanted to on the train, even in the aisles. The accompanying soldiers—one could not call them guards any longer— left us in peace. We were already being treated like free people.

On March 5, we came to the fort's center for special prisoners of war, created in January 1946. It was called "A School for Democracy." Before we were assigned to our quarters, one of our group was rejected because he was a member of the Nazi Party. He was a teacher, a good German, but he had been required under the Third Reich to join the Nazi Party, as all teachers in Germany were at the time.

A different war wind was blowing at Fort Eustis. There were no fences, only a sign in the grass warning people not to go farther. Our group was among the 2,000 POWs who were sent there each week for a six-day course. In all, 24,000 prisoners of war were brought to Fort Eustis to learn the basics of democracy.

Every morning the prisoners assembled in the auditorium to listen to lectures by various German professors about the United States government and geography and the English language. Each program began with the playing of Rossini's overture to *The Thieving Magpie*. We heard music by Felix Mendelssohn and Jacques Offenbach, long banned in Germany.

In the PX we could spend our daily wage of eighty cents on signs that adorned the walls. One read: "Democracy is not merely a governmental system, but a way of life." Another one, which could not be taken literally, said, "A woman's tongue is her sword, which she never lets rust."

At the end of our six-day course, we were directed to a classroom where the seats had been placed far apart from one another. Everyone was handed a pencil and some paper. A number of questions were thrown at us that we had to answer in one minute, such as "Why did Germany lose the war?" and "Will Germany have an army again in the future?" I gave them what I thought, not knowing what the future held for Germany, especially concerning an armed force.

The next morning, all 2,000 men assembled on a large field, and the names of those who should go to the right were called out. Mine was called, and the big question was, "Are we going home?" With great relief, I learned I had passed the test and could now return to my homeland.

Those who failed the exam, usually because they could not write fast enough, were re-examined. One fellow appeared before an American officer, who greeted him with "Heil Hitler!" The fellow answered with the same Nazi salute. The officer had one word for him: "Out!"

Quite a few of us who had parents and families now living in the Soviet Occupation Zone asked an American officer if we dared go home to that part of Germany. He almost got angry with us, saying, "What do you mean by that? The Russians are as good a people as we are."

He was right about the Russian people, but he had no idea what the Soviet leaders were really about. He should have known, but he was far away from there. I found out later, after my release, that many ex-prisoners ended up in the Soviet Union. They had used their discharge papers for a free ride home to that zone.

After our stay at Fort Eustis, we traveled to nearby Camp Patrick Henry, which was much smaller. Here we received twenty dollars. With this we bought cigarettes, tobacco, soap, or whatever we thought was a rarity in Germany. We were handed a certificate to prove we had obtained these items legally in case we were questioned later by German Customs.

At 2:30 p.m. on March 18, we left this camp looking quite respectable in our black-dyed uniforms with white PWs. Our train ride to New York State took us through Washington, D.C., where we all got a glimpse of the lighted dome of the Capitol building. That was a sight! The next morning we came to Camp Shanks, located on the Hudson River north of New York City.

We spent four days behind barbed wire again, then boarded a train that took us to New York Harbor. As I stood on a ferry passing the Statue of Liberty, I said to her, "I'll see you again some day." I knew then that I wanted to live in America.

Our ship, named the *Frederick Victory,* was moored and waiting for us. Before boarding, extreme caution was taken to make sure only those on the roster came on board. Then, at 8:30 a.m. on March 24, 1946, we left the United States of America.

Chapter Sixteen

A Country in Chaos

Strong currents caused by the Gulf Stream made the first days of our Atlantic crossing a bit rocky. Then the ocean became calm and we could be on deck any time we wanted. Once in a while we had to scrub the deck or do some painting, but otherwise we were on our own to enjoy the voyage.

The food on board was good and I saw five movies. Over the radio we learned that all German women who had been members of the Nazi Party were now being put to work in the cities, cleaning up bricks from the bombed-out houses. It was hard work for them, with not much to eat, but on hearing this we felt little compassion for them.

It was also around this time that we heard about the trials in Nuremberg, Germany. My buddies and I were very happy that all of these Nazi criminals were being put on trial. It was only too bad that Himmler, Goebbels, and Göring had already committed suicide. I would have liked to have seen them on the gallows.

On April 2, the European continent lay in front of us, but the fog at Le Havre, France, was so dense it delayed the ships entering the port. Our arrival time was 8:30 a.m. We finally disembarked at 1 p.m.

We rode by truck to a campsite in Bolbec. It was awful. The shelters we had for sleeping were worse than pigsties, and the food was terrible. Those of us from America had our own compound and kept away from the Polish guards, who wanted to get their hands on the "treasures" we had in our sacks. Our fine American transport commander saw to it that we were safe.

After a rather long march to the railway station, we left this infamous spot at 5:30 p.m. on April 4 and began our journey through France. We were traveling in freight cars with the doors open so we could jump out at the stations. At several places we faced encounters with French people.

One time a French-operated train filled with German POWs stopped on the tracks across from us. We were throwing American cigarettes to them, and one of the packages missed an open window and fell to the ground. A Frenchman picked it up and put it in his shirt pocket. One of the American guards saw this and motioned to the man to hand over the package to the POWs. He did so reluctantly after removing a few cigarettes. We applauded the guard with a heartfelt hand.

Another time, the French insisted that half of the occupants on our train be boarded onto a second train, supposedly for a difficult trek up a big hill ahead. Our train commander refused, suspecting the French wanted half of our men for themselves to work as slave laborers. "Don't be afraid," he told us. "Nothing will happen to you."

At 7 a.m. on April 6, we reached German soil, and the next day we arrived at our discharge camp in Bad Aibling, south of Munich. We received our discharge papers on April 11, and on the thirteenth I said goodbye to my friends with whom I had endured more pleasant than bad days.

I wasn't apprehensive about returning to Germany. I knew it would be ruined, but how ruined, I didn't know. As it was, the country was in chaos. Bridges were destroyed and buildings and churches demolished. There were shortages of food, clothing, and things like bicycle tires. I thought I could go to my parents' home in Lubmin, but there was no transportation to that town, so I was discharged to the Galena-Rucketts, family friends who lived north of Munich.

Rudolf and Alice Galena-Rucketts also had an apartment in New York, where he was an opera singer. They greeted me as though I were an angel. I was so welcome! Both were heavy smokers and I had American cigarettes, which made me even more popular. American cigarettes had much more value than the reichsmark; with this commodity, one could buy anything.

After three nights with the Galena-Rucketts, the police came to find me because I had not reported to the local police station. They told me to see an American officer at Munich City Hall who would help me with lodging, ration cards, and a job.

Because I had graduated from the School for Democracy, I was considered a special prisoner of war who was seen as trustworthy and who could be engaged in any kind of government work. It was funny—first I was branded as a traitor and then I was a hero!

The American officer arranged for my lodging with a retired schoolteacher in Munich. I was given work at an American military hospital as a janitor, waxing floors and cleaning brass. I was also a nurse's aide in a ward for shell-shocked Americans. It was sad to see them. Most had come from farms and were not accustomed to the rigorous discipline German soldiers were used to. Thank goodness, this job lasted only twelve days because the head nurse was a dragon. I told him that I had gotten better treatment as a prisoner.

I worked next in an American barracks for thirty days, peeling potatoes and washing kettles. I was able to get good food there. When lunch was over, I emptied the ashtrays and took the cigarette butts home. My landlord and I would recover all of the tobacco and make our own cigarettes. American cigarettes were expensive, at least ten marks. I could have bought the kingdom of Bavaria with my cigarettes.

One interesting thing was that nobody asked me about my experiences in the German Army or as a prisoner of war. No one wanted to talk about war, the Nazis, or Hitler. I think they wanted to forget.

The city of Munich was pretty much all rubble, and food was rationed except for potatoes. I had shattered a lens in my glasses while I was in New York and was lucky to find a pawn shop that had a lens that would fit. I was also given some clothing—a pair of pants that was much too big for me and looked like the pants to a tuxedo. Fortunately, my uniform was still in pretty good shape. A tailor altered it for me so the "PW" wouldn't show.

In the spring of 1946, my parents moved from Lubmin to East Berlin, where my father had been named head of dentistry at a former mental hospital. Most of the patients had been exterminated during the war, and now the facility served as a general hospital. My folks lived on the fourth floor of a house on the grounds. They were one of the few families to enjoy heat and hot water because the complex had its own power station. With the shortage of fuel, most Germans had to endure the cold.

My parents had no furniture, but were able to get a few pieces from the hospital. They told me the story of how my mother and sister—right after my family had fled Stettin—returned to get my father's dental instruments and also to pack up some toys and other belongings. They got out of Stettin in the last truck of the Gestapo, just ahead of the approaching Russians. My mother said to the driver, "The war is lost." She could have been shot as a traitor, but he agreed with her. The truck went into a ditch during the trip, and some of my Hummel figurines were damaged, but we saved more than most refugees.

I wanted to leave Munich and join my parents in East Berlin, but first my father had to get approval from the Soviet-controlled city. Finally, on July 7, the document arrived and, after a short quarantine in Leipzig, I was reunited with my folks on July 12.

(This was when I learned what had happened to the German POWs who had traveled free on their discharge papers directly to hometowns that were now controlled by the Soviets. Because these former soldiers had committed the Communist offense of serving in Hitler's army, they were transported to Russia to work for two years as slave laborers. Because I had traveled on my discharge papers to Munich, in the Allied sector, I was saved from this fate.)

Getting enough food was a problem for city people in Germany, while farmers could grow their own. If you saw people standing in line, you stood in line, too. But chances were that by the time you got to the front of the line, the bread or whatever it was had run out.

It was also impossible to get coffee beans—except through the black market—so most Germans made what was called *Ersatzkaffee* from such things as malted barley, potato peels, and chicory root. These substitutes for real coffee tasted terrible, but there was little choice.

In 1948, the Allies tried to feed the people of West Berlin through the famous Berlin airlift, which was truly a godsend. One of the commodities requested by the Germans was grain—meaning oats, rye, and wheat. In response, the Americans sent over cornmeal, which in Germany was not considered a food for people—only as chicken feed. So when the West Berliners received the cornmeal, they didn't know what to make of it.

To help with the shortage of food and fuel, West Berliners were allowed to have a free tree from that city's immense park. It looked like a battlefield, but a fair number of trees were still standing. People had to cut down the trees themselves, but then they could use them for fuel or to barter for other goods. My sister, who had moved to West Berlin, paid to have a tree cut down, then she used it to barter for food.

Chapter Seventeen

"Don't Forget Your Homeland"

I knew I had to get away from menial work, that I had to go to school. I read a book about the Amazon written by a naturalist/photographer. It intrigued me so much that I was inspired to become a photographer myself. My father always liked to take pictures and this added to my enthusiasm.

First, I thought I should improve my English, so I enrolled in an English course in West Berlin. Before the Berlin Wall went up in 1961, people could travel back and forth between East Berlin and West Berlin. I was disappointed, though, with the instructor—he had no idea about American English. He wanted to teach British English. It helped, but at the end of the course I felt like I was still in children's shoes.

In the spring of 1947, I applied to Lette Verein, a school in West Berlin that taught photography. Because I was a former soldier, I was immediately accepted but had to wait for an opening that August. It took two hours by el train to go from my parent's home in East Berlin to downtown West Berlin. There was no glass in the train windows, so in the winter I didn't sit much. Instead, I walked around to keep warm. Once I reached my stop, I walked for another twenty or thirty minutes to the school. The building had sustained a lot of damage, and the teacher had a little electric stove to try to keep us warm.

It was a two-year program, but I got sick in 1949 and missed graduation. The doctor didn't know what I had, so I was put in isolation in the hospital. My mother came every day.

Suddenly I was into poetry. I wrote a poem each day and read it to my mother. The poems were about the food, what they did to me in the hospital, things like that. Afterwards, I typed them all up and gave them to my parents. When I graduated on February 15, 1950, I wrote a long poem about the school. Then, over the years, the impulse subsided.

My first job was darkroom worker for a Jewish photographer in East Berlin named Hans Heineman. I did all the photo finishing and worked with children who were having their pictures taken. He couldn't handle the children and I could.

But I wanted a job with better pay and more responsibility. I visited the Labor Office in East Berlin. My employer's son—who was an official in the Communist youth movement—cautioned me, "You will never get a good job from them because you were in America and could be a spy." Then I quit my job, realizing I couldn't get anywhere under the Communists.

I had a darkroom at home and made postcards from pictures I had of Stettin. People who used to live there were happy to buy them. I also took pictures for the owner of a small photo store. When he had a job for me to do, he would let me know by putting out a little flag.

On February 10, 1952, my parents and I attended a festival in West Berlin, sort of like a Mardi Gras. A big family was gathered at one of the tables, where there was this cute girl wearing an ivory-colored hat. I saw a guy sit down next to her, and I thought, "There goes that." But then I learned he was her brother. A woman at the festival knew that the girl's mother and my mother had gone to school together fifty years earlier, and she made introductions all around. I asked the girl to dance. I learned that her name was Walburg Hildebrandt and that she was working as a dietician in an old folks' home. She had studied home economics in school.

The following Sunday she came to a festival in West Berlin hosted by my "hometown circle," a large group of us whose hometown was Stettin. She was nice—just the right girl I was looking for. As it turned out, she was looking for something permanent, too. My father and mother fell in love with her immediately. We were engaged on December 2, 1952, and married on June 12, 1953. We were married by a magistrate in the morning and in a church in the afternoon. We settled into one room in my mother-in-law's apartment in Berlin-Steglitz.

A friend of mine took this picture of my beautiful future bride, Walburg Hildebrandt, during the evening I met her, February 10, 1952.

Before the wedding, it had taken four trips for me to sneak all of my belongings into West Berlin because it was a crime under the Communists to move into that Allied-occupied city. Walburg had lived north of Koszalin right on the Baltic Sea, but in 1936 moved with her family to West Berlin because during World War I her father had been with the German air force and Göring wanted him back. As it turned out, she was my passport to America now that I, too, was living in West Berlin.

I applied for an identification card with the West Berlin authorities and went on unemployment. Walburg became a cook in a beer brewery, where she worked until 1954. In the meantime I got a job at an American-operated studio in the town of Hanau, east of Frankfurt, where American soldiers could get their pictures taken. Eventually, she joined me there and worked again at an old folks' home.

Conditions in Germany during the 1950s were bad. The cities were still in shambles and the housing situation was bleak. To get better housing, one had to have a certain number of points, and we were far away from that. We made the best of our situation, but I wasn't very hopeful about the future. I wished to return to America.

In 1956 I found out through a colleague that an organization called Church World Service was working with the United States government to help displaced persons emigrate to America. I told Walburg about it that evening, saying, "It's time to leave." She agreed. Up to this point, she had not been very enthused about leaving Germany.

We wrote to the organization's office in Hamburg and received a letter that said, "Yes, we would like to help you." We had to send them our police and health records. Then an American who spoke German came to see us with a long questionnaire.

On October 26, 1956, my wife gave birth to our first child, Dorothea Elisabeth. We were more anxious than ever to go to America.

Later that year, we were informed that we had a sponsor in New York City. I replied that we didn't want to go to New York City— joking that "New York City isn't America." My first choice was either Michigan or Illinois. Then, in January 1957, we received a letter that we were to report to Hamburg on January 20 because we were going to America. We were jubilant! It was a happy day!

As excited as we were, it was a difficult time for our families, who were sad about our leaving. My mother tried to be strong and said, "Whatever you do in your life is all right with me." I remember my father saying, "Don't forget your homeland."

We left Germany by airplane on January 23, arriving in New York City the morning of January 24. We were told we were going to Michigan and that our sponsor was All Saints Episcopal Church in East Lansing. I was so happy at the thought of living in this state.

From New York, we traveled by train to Michigan on the same

route that I had taken as a POW in 1944—only this time we continued
a little north of Battle Creek to East Lansing.

When we got off the train, members of the church met us
with smiles and hugs. They did everything they could to make
our transition easy. We felt that we had "hit the jackpot" with this
wonderful congregation. We also met other people in the Lansing
area who had come from Germany. One of the nicest things we found
about settling in America was that no one ever said an unkind word to
us because we were German.

Our first apartment was on the first floor of a house at 113
Clemens Street in Lansing; the house is still there. The church paid
our first eight months' rent and gave us clothes and other things for
the baby. The apartment was small and spartan, but more than what
we had in Germany, which was not only small, but cold in the winter
and hot in the summer.

After only four days, I had a job in photography. A man named
Norm Shaver owned a studio in East Lansing and needed a printer to
develop his pictures. Later he consolidated with Kowalski Studios on
Michigan Avenue in Lansing. I printed all of the senior pictures for
Okemos High School and the Lansing high schools.

We lived close to many shops and found the A & P store to be
especially interesting. Food was in abundance. Marshmallows! We
had never seen them before. We also discovered pie and strawberry
shortcake, which we did not have in Germany. Popcorn was new to
us, too.

In September, the church found a new home for us on North
Harrison in East Lansing. The landlord was very happy to have us. It
was a two-story house with a garage and a nice yard with lots of oak
trees. I was able to convert a little room into a darkroom. We would
take long walks with the baby buggy. One time we thought we would
walk all the way to the Capitol building in downtown Lansing—
four miles—but we gave up before we got there. We were always
exploring.

I was interested in learning as much English as possible. My boss
and some German friends told me to listen to the radio and read *The
Saturday Evening Post* and *Reader's Digest*. I would listen every day
to WKAR from Michigan State University in East Lansing and to
WJR out of Detroit.

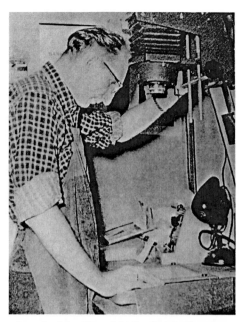

I worked for Kowalski Studios in Lansing, Michigan, from February 1957 to December 1963. I printed about thirty high school senior portraits a day in black and white, all by hand.

That spring, my wife and I decided to enroll in English as a Second Language classes at Lansing Community College. The first night, the instructor had trouble pronouncing Walburg's name and said she would call her "Barbara." From then on, my wife introduced herself to everyone as Barbara. I think I was the only one in America who continued to call her Walburg.

One time in class we were asked to write a description of a picture on the wall. Later, the teacher told me she was so intrigued by my writing that she had shown it to the other teachers. That made me very happy.

We had a garage on North Harrison, but no car. Besides, I didn't know how to drive. In 1959, I enrolled in a driver education course at Lansing Community College and, after finishing the class, taught my wife how to drive. Then we bought our first automobile, a 1953 green Chevy. We were beginning to live the American dream.

Chapter Eighteen

Small-Town America

Our family was growing. Our second daughter, Cornelia Amalie, was born on May 25, 1958, and our son, Dietrich Glasenap, was born on September 9, 1959. We needed a bigger house. And even though I had a nice job and Walburg was making all of the clothes for our children, I knew I needed to earn more money.

A community called Grand Ledge, about twelve miles west of Lansing, seemed like the perfect spot for us. With only 5,000 souls, it was what we thought of as "small-town America." We also liked its natural beauty, with the Grand River running through it and sandstone ledges rising up from the banks.

In 1960, we bought a house on Bridge Street, where I set up my own photography business. We were located just one-and-a-half blocks from the main intersection and close to everything—churches, stores, restaurants, the movie house, and the river with a big island. The kids would be able to walk to school. It was ideal.

The pastor from the Methodist church came to our home and gave us his blessing. We also had a visit from the Lutheran minister. A local radio station interviewed me, and the *Grand Ledge Independent* wrote a big story about us.

I was the only photographer in Grand Ledge at the time, and high schools in the area hired me to take senior pictures. I was also taking every other kind of picture—weddings, children, groups, portraits, even pets. From the beginning, the most important thing to me was that my customers were happy.

I wanted to become involved in the community, and the first thing I joined was the Jaycees. Over the years, I also became a member of the Grand Ledge Chamber of Commerce, served on the board of the Grand Ledge Historical Society, became president of the PTA at our children's school, and served as both secretary and president of the Grand Ledge Rotary Club.

My wife was a very talented singer as well as seamstress. She sang in the choral group at Michigan State University and was the soloist for Handel's *Messiah* in a special Christmas program. She made beautiful bobbin lace; some of her work adorns the altar of The Peoples Church of East Lansing. She also volunteered for many years at Woldumar Nature Center near Grand Ledge, dressing up in period costume to demonstrate bobbin lacemaking at the historic log cabin there.

We had to wait five years from the time we arrived in America to apply for citizenship. We made application in early spring, 1962. My wife attended citizenship classes for a few weeks at Lansing Community College, and I learned from her.

Ironically, it was on Hitler's birthday, April 20, that we had to go to Grand Rapids, Michigan, for an interview to see if we were qualified. We had to bring character witnesses with us. One of the questions was, "What does the word 'democracy' mean to you?" I told them, "Democracy is not merely a form of government; it is a form of living." The sign with that message on it at Fort Eustis had made a lasting impression on me.

In June, we got a letter in the mail telling us that we had become American citizens. I was thirty-seven years old; my wife, thirty-eight. We were so happy. The first thing we did was go out and buy an American flag to fly from the front of our home.

One of my favorite assignments as a photographer in Grand Ledge was taking pictures for our local BoarsHead Theater. Sadly, it is now closed, but it held the distinction of being the oldest professional theater in Mid-Michigan. Many actors came through here before they made it big, including William Hurt, Mary Beth Hurt, and John Heard. As the theater photographer, I was able to meet all of them. One time, my wife, who worked in the theater's costume shop, mended William Hurt's pants.

The highlight of my life took place in 1975, when the mayor of Grand Ledge asked me to be chairman of the city's Bicentennial Committee. The members were all nice people and we had fun. Our most important undertaking was raising $5,000 to build a pavilion on the island in time for the celebration. We held an auction and also sold special buttons. Some good guys here in town built the pavilion; we all worked on it. Meanwhile, my wife was busy making colonial costumes for us, including a tricorne hat for me.

On the day of the celebration, July 4, 1976, I had to give a speech for the first time in my life. It went over well; better than I thought it would. People came up to me afterward and said, "I never thought you could do this." My wife and I were given a carriage ride through town, and there was a big party that night with fireworks. We had a great time.

Walburg and I dressed in colonial costumes so we could celebrate the July 4, 1976, American Bicentennial in style. She designed and sewed both of our outfits, including my tricorne hat.

We found living in the United States so pleasant that we wanted to see more of it. We took many trips, from New England to New Mexico. One of the books at Camp Hatch included a map of the United States, and I had learned about the different states from that. We also traveled overseas. In 1992, on a trip to Germany, I showed Walburg my hometown, which is now part of Poland and called "Szczecin." I had not seen Stettin since April 2, 1944. While the city has been beautifully rebuilt, we could still see bomb damage to the side of the hospital.

My wife passed away in 1997. She was beside me as we were crossing the main street in Grand Ledge. We could see no cars coming, when suddenly I felt a car hit me in the shoulder, knocking me to the ground. I came back to my senses in an ambulance and was told she was on the way to the hospital, too. The police called our children.

After two days, she slipped into a coma. Her head was covered and she was hooked up to lots of tubes; she looked bad. Three days went by. We were all there—our pastor, too, as he had come to see us every day. The doctor came into the room and said there was no hope. We agreed as a family to shut off her life support.

My right leg had been completely shattered below the knee. The surgeon saved my leg and mended my shoulder with an iron rod and pins. An MRI showed that my brain was okay, but I had to have stitches where my head had hit the windshield. I went to my wife's funeral in a wheelchair, a cast on my leg. After three weeks of physical rehabilitation, I came home.

My wife was a great mother to our three children and a wonderful grandmother for our grandsons, Neil and George. Quite a few pictures of her brighten the walls of my living room. A plaque with her picture graces a wall in the log cabin at Woldumar Nature Center, honoring her contributions to the center and to the people who learned from her there.

I remain active in the Grand Ledge community, playing the harmonica and pan flute for Christmas celebrations, riverboat cruises, parades, and the annual art fair. And I may be the only American with a heavy German accent to play Uncle Sam in a Fourth of July parade. I have been "Uncle Sam" in Grand Ledge's summer festivities since 1994.

*The people of Grand Ledge have come
to know that I am "Uncle Sam" in our
Yankee Doodle Days Parade.*

For two years I dressed up as the Easter Bunny for the Grand
Ledge Easter parade, but the furry costume was too hot and I asked
that someone else take over that honor.

I have also participated since the 1960s in Michigan's famous
Mackinac Bridge Walk. The five-mile-long bridge, completed in 1957
to connect the Upper and Lower peninsulas, is one of Michigan's
treasures. The walk is held every year on Labor Day and led by the
governor of our state. The year 2013 marked the sixteenth time I
joined the bridge walk. My son, Dietrich, a professional photographer
in Traverse City, Michigan, has taken pictures of the bridge from its
tall towers. I can remember one year how exciting it was for my wife
and me to see him way up high with his photography equipment. I
am also very proud that a greatly enlarged photo of the bridge walk

taken by Dietrich is on display at the Michigan Historical Museum in Lansing.

In 2003, I was invited to speak at Ramstein Air Base in Rhineland-Palatinate, Germany, which is the headquarters of U.S. Air Forces in Europe. The base was holding its annual ceremony honoring POWs and MIAs. I considered the invitation itself to be an honor. Over two days, September 18-19, I talked to four different groups about my experiences as a German soldier and as a prisoner of war in America. Afterwards, they showered me with gifts, including two books about the Berlin airlift, a beer mug, a pewter plate, and commemorative coins.

In 2010, my daughter Nellie and I traveled to Germany. During the trip, while Nellie was visiting my wife's sisters, I decided to see for myself one of the remainders of the horrors committed by the Nazis. I took a tour of Sachsenhausen Concentration Camp in the town of Oranienburg, thirty-five kilometers north of Berlin. It was one of the first camps to hold political prisoners; later, it was used to imprison anyone the Nazis believed to be "inferior." I wandered around where the inmates lived, knowing that most of them didn't survive. I didn't have a very good feeling, but I told myself that it was history.

I continue to take trips, particularly to other countries through an overseas tour company. My most recent trip was to Germany and Poland with my three children in September 2013. I have also visited Chile, Costa Rica, the Czech Republic, Ecuador, Egypt, Guatemala, Mexico, Morocco, Nepal, New Zealand, and Peru.

Most of the time, however, you can find me around town, taking part in community activities and happily making the best of life with my family and friends.

If you ever go to Grand Ledge's Sun Theatre to watch a movie, just before the previews you will see a big advertisement filling the screen: "Yes, I Am Still in Business. Ernst Floeter, Photographer."

Epilogue

My Guardian Angel

My homeland is a country of great natural beauty, with majestic forests, graceful rivers, and glorious mountains. It also has a distinguished cultural heritage in music, literature, philosophy, and architecture. I am proud to be German.

But I am not proud of what happened under Hitler. Because of him, Germany lost its honor. I am thankful that its prestige in the world is rising, but this will continue only so long as Germans do not deny what happened.

When I returned to Germany in 1946, no one would talk about the war. People were trying just to survive, with terrible deprivations. It wasn't until 1957 when I saw a television program with Walter Cronkite that I fully understood about the concentration camps and the other atrocities committed throughout Europe.

My family was lucky. My parents and sister survived. The only thing they lost were possessions, and so they ended up better off than most. They started a new life and tried to make the best of it.

For me, I felt the presence of a guardian angel looking over me, from the time I entered boot camp until I returned to Germany as a free man. If any one decision or event had been different, I easily could have been one of the millions who perished during that horrific time. Because of my guardian angel, I survived, and so I'm glad I lived through that time. I have all of these memories.

As much as I love America, I have never lost sight of my roots.

My wife and I named our children after family members and spoke German to them from the time they were born. Today, all three can speak German and English. As a child in Germany, I learned to love all types of music, but German marches continue to be my favorite. I enjoy books and movies about Germany, too, and I subscribe to several German-language newspapers to stay current with news about my homeland.

I have no family left in Germany, but I am glad my father was able to visit America in 1965 and 1972, and my sister, in 1990. My mother, Elisabeth Glasenap Floeter, passed away in 1971, and my father, Dr. Ernst Herman Floeter, in 1976. My sister, Gisela Margarete Elisabeth Floeter, four years older than I, died in 2010.

My wife and I traveled to Berlin for Gisela's funeral and to secure family heirlooms. We brought back to America more than 1,000 pounds of furniture, books, photos, and other mementos, including my childhood briefcase and a rare picture of my father when he was in high school. I feel so lucky to have these treasures to pass on to my own children.

Perhaps because I have had a fortunate life, I feel a deep obligation to explain to Americans why the German people should not be blamed for the unspeakable crimes committed by the Nazis—but, rather, how they became totally defenseless under Hitler's murderous regime. I have given talks before civic clubs, schools, churches, Boy Scout troops, military groups, and ethnic organizations about the fundamental goodness of the German people. It was an especial honor for me to speak at the United States Holocaust Memorial Museum in Washington, D.C., on May 19, 2012. I continue to give talks to this day.

Serving as a prisoner of war was a significant part of my life, and, despite the circumstances, I met a lot of nice people during that time. I have tried to contact not only comrades, but also guards and the farmers I worked for.

One of my best buddies, Thomas Kramer, moved to the southwestern part of Germany when he returned home in 1946. We exchanged letters and got together in 1976 during one of my trips to Germany. Over the years, we lost contact and I am not sure whether he is still alive.

I have been back to Hatch, New Mexico, fifteen or sixteen times since moving to Michigan. My wife and I always enjoyed the trip down there. I learned the town is known as the "Chile Capital of the World" and hosts a two-day chile festival each year in early September. I also found out that the calaboose—our "jail" at camp—still exists and is locked up in a restricted area on the Las Cruces fairgrounds.

We made our first visit to New Mexico in 1977 on our way back from taking our daughter Dorothea to Fort Huachuca in Cochise County, Arizona. She had joined the U.S. Army. (I am proud to say that Dorothea retired in June 2013 as a master sergeant.) We stopped in Hatch and found a motel that had been there in 1945 and 1946. We toured the town and learned that Mr. Johnston, the bank president, was residing in an old folks' home. The small house we had built for him out of cinder blocks was still standing.

We also found Mr. Mundy's farm—he was the farmer who taught me how to hoe weeds—and met his grandson, Joe Morrow. Mr. Mundy had passed away by then. We were treated very graciously by Joe and his wife, Bobbie. I have visited them many times since then and am happy to call them my friends.

In November of 1959, my wife and I took our first trip to Fort Custer National Cemetery in Battle Creek, Michigan, where a ceremony is held each year to honor twenty-six German prisoners of war who died at Fort Custer. Sixteen were killed in a train-truck collision and ten died of natural causes. Called *Volkstrauertag*, it is a beautiful ceremony, with flags, wreaths, speeches, and singing by a German chorus. I have gone every year. In 2013, Oskar Schmoling and I were the only two former prisoners of war at Fort Custer left to attend. Oskar had been the youngest POW at the camp.

At one of these ceremonies, I was happy to see a former guard named Fred Spencer. I remembered him well because he had a little dog at Camp Hatch. In one of my early trips to Hatch, I met a relative of his who gave me his address. I learned that he lived in Michigan (of all places) in a little town northeast of Kalamazoo called Richland. I eagerly wrote to him, and he said he would meet me at Fort Custer. After that first reunion, my wife and I visited him at his home several times, and once he traveled to Grand Ledge to ours.

About ten years ago, I found the poem I had written in 1950 about my photography school. I sent it to the school, explaining that I had been a student there right after the war. In 2010, my daughter Nellie and I traveled to Berlin. I wanted her to see my old school. We were greeted by the teachers, and I told them I was the one who had sent the poem. They said they had placed it in their archives and were very happy to have it. While I was there, they asked me if I could help them identify the photo of a former student from my era. What a coincidence—I told them the picture was of me!

Although I have reached out to old acquaintances and maintain a heartfelt interest in my homeland, I always live in the present. It took eleven years for me to realize my dream of returning to the United States and I am grateful every day to be living here.

I am proud to be an American.

Glossary

Selected Terms of World War II

Afrika Korps: The German expeditionary force that fought in North Africa under Field Marshal Erwin Rommel. It surrendered to Allied forces in May 1943.

Allied Powers: The nations opposing the Axis powers. The major Allies were the United Kingdom, France, the United States, and the Soviet Union. The others were Australia, Belgium, Brazil, Canada, China, Czechoslovakia, Ethiopia, Greece, India, Mexico, the Netherlands, Newfoundland, New Zealand, Norway, South Africa, and Yugoslavia.

Aryan: The term used by the Nazis to refer to Caucasians with a northern European heritage, whom they considered to be the "master race."

Atomic Age: The era of nuclear technology ushered in with the first testing of an atomic bomb in July 1945 and the bombing of Hiroshima and Nagasaki, Japan, in August of that year.

Auschwitz Concentration Camp: The largest of the concentration camps under the Third Reich. Located in Nazi-controlled Poland, it consisted of three main camps and a number of satellite camps.

Axis Powers: The nations—Germany, Italy, and Japan—that fought the Allied powers.

BBC: The British Broadcasting Corporation, established by the British government in 1922. During the war, it sought to reach listeners in Germany and Occupied Europe with radio broadcasts about the progression of the war and the evils of the Nazi government.

Beer Hall Putsch: Adolf Hitler's first attempt to orchestrate a Nazi revolution (*putsch*) in Germany. On November 8, 1923, he announced his intentions at a Munich beer hall rally and the next day led his stormtroopers in an unsuccessful effort to seize the Bavarian government.

Bulge, Battle of the: A major German offensive begun in December 1944 against Allied forces in France, Luxembourg, and Belgium. It ended in January 1945 in a decisive victory for the Allies.

Church World Service: A Christian-based organization founded in 1946 to assist persons displaced by the war. Over the years it has expanded its mission to include disaster relief, the eradication of hunger and poverty, and the promotion of human rights, among other objectives.

Cronkite, Walter (1916-2009): A legendary American broadcast journalist best known as the CBS television evening news anchorman from 1962 to 1981. From 1953 to 1957, he hosted "You Are There," a CBS program that brought historical events to life.

Dachau Concentration Camp: The first concentration camp (1933) created in Germany by the Nazi government. Located north of Munich at a former munitions factory, it originally housed political prisoners. The population grew over time to include criminals, Jews, and other persons deemed "inferior."

Danzig: An independently governed city on the Baltic Sea seized by Nazi Germany in 1939. After World War II, it was given to Poland and is now called Gdansk.

D-Day: June 6, 1944, the day the Allied forces invaded German-occupied France at Normandy.

Deutsches Jungvolk: Meaning "German Youth," it was a subdivision of Hitler Youth that recruited boys ages ten to fourteen. Participants were taught loyalty to Adolf Hitler and the importance of physical fitness.

Deutschland: Germany

Deutschmark: The monetary unit of Germany from 1948 to 1999, when it was replaced by the euro.

Displaced Persons: Those who could not return to their homes or homelands after the war. Included were survivors of concentration camps and slave labor camps, former prisoners of war, orphans, and Germans who were forced to flee regions no longer controlled by Nazi Germany.

East Berlin: The eastern portion of the city of Berlin controlled by the Soviet Union after the war. East Berlin served as capital of Soviet-controlled East Germany until 1990, when East Germany and West Germany were reunited.

East Germany: The area of occupied Germany controlled by the Soviet Union from June 1945 until October 1990.

Eisenhower, Dwight D. (1890-1969): A five-star general in the U.S. Army and supreme commander of the Allied Forces in Europe. After the war, he was elected U. S. president in 1952 and again in 1956.

Führer: The title adopted by Adolf Hitler, meaning "leader."

Gestapo: The Nazi secret police force known for its extreme brutality. Gestapo agents routinely arrested people suspected of being disloyal to the Nazi government and sent them to concentration camps.

Goebbels, Joseph (1897-1945): Adolf Hitler's propaganda minister, who controlled all of Germany's communication channels, including radio, newspapers, and motion pictures. His pro-Nazi, anti-Semitic messages were designed to promote German loyalty to the Nazi government and create animosity toward Jews.

Göring, Hermann (1893-1946): Commander of the Luftwaffe, Nazi Germany's air force. Göring was responsible for building up Germany's war machine prior to the start of the war.

Hague Conventions: International agreements defining the rules of warfare, signed in 1899 and 1907 at The Hague, Netherlands. A third convention planned for 1914 did not take place because of the outbreak of World War I.

Hague, The: The seat of government of the Netherlands and site of the Hague Conventions.

Heydrich, Reinhard (1904-1942): The third-highest Nazi official after Adolf Hitler and Heinrich Himmler. Known as the "Butcher of Prague," Heydrich was the chief architect of the Holocaust and was considered the most cold-blooded figure in the Nazi administration. He died on June 4, 1942, following a bomb attack on his automobile outside Prague, Czechoslovakia.

Himmler, Heinrich (1900-1945): The Nazi military commander in charge of the SS (*Schutzstaffel*). Second in command after Hitler, Himmler was also overseer of Germany's concentration camps and responsible for directing the extermination of more than six million Jews and millions of other civilians.

Hindenburg: The most famous of the passenger-carrying airships manufactured in Germany during the 1930s. The LZ 129 *Hindenburg* took its first flight on March 4, 1936. It was destroyed by fire on May 6, 1937, while landing at Lakehurst Naval Air Station in New Jersey.

Hindenburg, Paul von (1847-1934): Second president of the Weimar Republic from 1925 until his death. In 1933, he was induced to appoint Adolf Hitler chancellor.

Hirohito (1901-1989): Emperor of Japan from 1926 until his death. He was head of state during Japan's participation in the war as an Axis power.

Hitler, Adolf (1889-1945): Chancellor of Germany from 1933 until his death, and very likely the most reviled person in human history. His policies and actions are considered the main causes of World War II.

Hitler Youth: The official Nazi youth organization. Its purpose was to indoctrinate German boys, ages fourteen to eighteen, in Nazi ideology and prepare them for military service.

Holocaust: The mass extermination by the Nazi government of more than six million Jews. The term is sometimes also used to refer to the millions of other civilians killed by the Nazis.

Kristallnacht: "Night of Broken Glass." On November 9-10, 1938, the Nazi government provoked the mass destruction of synagogues and Jewish-owned shops throughout Germany and parts of Austria.

Nearly one hundred Jews were killed and thousands were sent to concentration camps.

Kaiser: Meaning "emperor," it was the term used by rulers of the German Empire from 1871 to the end of World War I in 1918.

LSTs: Tank transport ships that carried tanks directly onto beaches along with troops and all of the needed combat gear. LST stands for "Landing Ship, Tank."

Machine pistol: A hand-held automatic gun with a high rate of fire.

MASH unit: The abbreviation for Mobile Army Surgical Hospital. MASH units serve in war combat areas to treat wounded soldiers quickly.

Munich Agreement: The pact allowing Germany to annex the Sudetenland in western Czechoslovakia. The agreement was signed on September 30, 1938, by Great Britain, France, and Italy following Hitler's demand that Germans living in Czechoslovakia be reunited with their homeland.

Mussolini, Benito (1883-1945): The Fascist dictator of Italy, one of the Axis powers, from 1922 until his ouster in 1943. Known as *Il Duce* (the leader), he was executed in 1945.

Mustangs: Fighter bombers of the U.S. Army Air Corps during the war.

Nazi Party (also called the **National Socialist German Workers' Party**): The political party of Adolf Hitler that appeared in Germany in 1920. Nazis believed in extreme nationalism; militarism; the expansion of Germany's borders; and the persecution of Jews, others considered to be inferior, and those who did not agree with Nazi ideology.

Normandy: Site of the June 6, 1944, Allied invasion of occupied France. The region is situated in northern France along the English Channel coast.

Nuremberg Trials: A series of trials that brought Nazi war criminals to justice for war crimes, crimes against humanity, and crimes against peace. These military tribunals were held in Nuremberg, Germany, between 1945 and 1949.

Pyle, Ernie (1900-1945): An American newspaperman who wrote a popular syndicated column about World War II. He traveled with U.S. troops in Europe and throughout the Pacific, where he was killed on April 18, 1945, by Japanese machine-gun fire.

Reich: German term for "kingdom" or "empire."

Reichsarbeitsdienst: The Reich Labor Service, a compulsory public works program for young German men and women who had reached the age of eighteen. Participants carried out such tasks as building airstrips, repairing roads, draining marshes, and planting trees.

Reichsmark: The monetary unit of Germany from 1924 until 1948, when it was replaced by the deutschmark.

Rommel, Erwin (1891-1944): A German field marshal best known for leading the Afrika Korps in the North African Campaign in Algeria, Egypt, Libya, Morocco, and Tunisia in 1941-43. Rommel was forced to die by poison for his part in the July 20, 1944, plot to assassinate Adolf Hitler.

Roosevelt, Franklin D. (1882-1945): President of the United States from March 1933 until his death of a cerebral hemorrhage in April 1945. He brought America into World War II on December 8, 1941, the day after the Japanese attacked Pearl Harbor in the U. S. Hawaiian Islands.

Sachsenhausen Concentration Camp: A Nazi concentration camp in the town of Oranienburg, located thirty-five kilometers north of Berlin. It was created in 1936 primarily for political prisoners. Later, Jews, criminals, and homosexuals were also imprisoned and executed there.

SS or **Schutzstaffel:** An elite force that served as Adolf Hitler's personal security guard as well as a security force throughout Germany and the occupied countries. It was responsible for committing many of the crimes against humanity that took place during the war.

Silesia: A region in the southwestern part of Poland. Following World War I, Upper Silesia was included in the new nation of Poland, and Germany continued its control of Lower Silesia. With the conquest of Poland in 1939, Germany once again gained Upper Silesia. It was restored to Poland at war's end.

Soviet Occupation Zone: The eastern part of Germany occupied by the Soviet Union at the end of the war. The region became East Germany, with East Berlin as its capital. East Germany and West Germany—the latter controlled by the Allied nations of the United Kingdom, France, and the U.S.—were reunited on October 3, 1990.

Stalingrad, Battle of: The German Army's attempt to capture the Soviet city of Stalingrad. Considered one of the bloodiest battles in world history, it began in August 1942 and ended in February 1943 as a victory for the Soviets, effectively stopping Germany's eastward advance.

Stettin: Germany's largest port on the Baltic Sea prior to 1945. During the war, Allied bombing and, later, fierce fighting between German and Soviet forces destroyed more than sixty-five percent of the city. When Stettin fell to the Soviets in April 1945, most of the German inhabitants fled. In a post-war agreement, Stettin was given to Poland and renamed "Szczecin."

Sudetenland: An ethnically German region in western Czechoslovakia annexed by Adolf Hitler through the Munich Agreement in 1938. After the war, the area was returned to Czechoslovakia and the German population was ejected.

Swastika: An ancient symbol depicting a cross with the ends of its arms bent at right angles in a clockwise direction. The Nazi Party adopted it as its symbol in 1920.

Third Geneva Convention: One of four international agreements regarding the lawful conduct of war. The Third Geneva Convention, adopted in 1929, defines the humane treatment of prisoners of war.

Third Reich: Nazi Germany, under the chancellorship of Adolf Hitler, from 1933 to 1945. The First Reich was that of the Holy Roman Empire from the tenth century to 1806. The Second Reich was the Hohenzollern (or German Empire) period from 1871 to 1918.

VE-Day: Victory in Europe Day, May 8, 1945—the day the Allies accepted Nazi Germany's unconditional surrender.

Versailles, Treaty of: The peace treaty signed after World War I, on June 28, 1919. The harsh conditions imposed on Germany are considered the principal reasons the Nazi Party was able to rise in popularity. Under the treaty, Germany had to give up territory to Belgium, Czechoslovakia, Denmark, France, and Poland; relinquish its overseas colonies; make substantial war reparations; reduce its armed forces to 100,000; and give up most of its armaments.

Volkstrauertag: A day set aside in Germany to remember the soldiers who died in World Wars I and II as well as those who died as a result of violent oppression. The annual commemoration, held the second from the last Sunday before the first day of Advent, includes speeches, prayers, and the laying of wreaths.

West Berlin: The western half of the city of Berlin controlled after the war by France, the United Kingdom, and the United States. West Berlin was considered a West German city until 1990, when East Germany and West Germany were reunited.

West Germany: The area in postwar Germany comprised of three zones occupied, respectively, by the United States, the United Kingdom, and France until October 1990.

Wilhelm II (1859-1941): The last kaiser to rule Germany. He abdicated in November 1918 at the end of World War I (before the armistice was signed) and fled to the Netherlands, where he lived in exile until his death.

World War I (also known as the **Great War**): A global war that began on July 28, 1914, with the assassination of Archduke Franz Ferdinand of Austria and ended November 11, 1918, with the surrender of Germany.

World War II: A global war that began on September 1, 1939, with the German invasion of Poland and ended September 2, 1945, with the surrender of Japan.

CPSIA information can be obtained at www.ICGtesting.com
Printed in the USA
BVOW07s1517210814

363562BV00001B/85/P

9 781595 945365